Street Children

A Guide to Effective Ministry

Phyllis Kilbourn, editor

MARC

800 West Chestnut Avenue, Monrovia, California 91016-3198 USA

Street Children
A Guide to Effective Ministry
Phyllis Kilbourn, editor

ISBN 1-887983-01-5

Published by MARC, a division of World Vision International, 800 West Chestnut Avenue, Monrovia, California 91016-3198 U.S.A.

Printed in the United States of America. Editor and typesetter: Edna G. Valdez. Cover design: Richard Sears. Cover photo: Street child in Lima, Peru. Latin America Mission photo by Samuel Nieva.

Contents

Contributing Authors

Alemtsehai Alemu. From Addis Ababa, Ethiopia. Completed undergraduate studies in economics at Addis Ababa University and earned a Master of Philosophy degree from the University of Strathclyde in Glasgow, Scotland. Currently country coordinator for Dorcas Aid International's Ethiopia projects that focus on intervention care for street children.

Jeff Anderson. Graduate of St. Cloud University, U.S.A., with a degree in sociology and criminal justice studies. Worked for Midwest Challenge, a Christ-centered drug and alcohol rehabilitation program, from 1977 to 1984. He and his wife began their ministry in Manila, the Philippines, with Action International Ministries in 1985, where they are involved in ministry to street children in metro Manila. The Andersons also coordinated an extensive relief and development project for many of the Mt. Pinatubo volcano victims.

Tony Culnane. Researcher and campaigns adviser for World Vision Australia, with particular responsibilities for issues concerning children, refugees, persons with disabilities and urbanization. During 1993-95, he served as the inaugural manager of World Vision International's Cambodia street children project in Phnom Penh. Extensive background in counseling and academic qualifications in theology, pastoral ministry, clinical pastoral counseling and community counseling.

Cynthia Blomquist Eriksson. Clinical psychology doctoral student at Fuller Theological Seminary Graduate School of Psychology, Pasadena, U.S.A. Also working toward a M.A. in theology with an emphasis in cross-cultural studies. Currently doing internship for her Ph.D. at a veteran's administrative outpatient clinic in Los Angeles, where she is involved in group and individual therapy and assessment of post-traumatic stress disorder (PTSD) with former combatants.

Michael DiPaolo. Currently in Ph.D. program in clinical psychology at the California School of Professional Psychology,

v

U.S.A. Masters degree in developmental psychology from Columbia University/Teachers College in New York. Served in leadership and supervisory roles with Covenant House, a Catholic outreach to street children, in Texas and California. Presently doing his internship at Pacific Clinic, a community mental health clinic for individuals and families. Also coordinates spiritual development activities for young adults at his church.

Perry Downs. Ph.D. from New York University. Professor of Christian education and director of the doctor of education program at Trinity International University, Deerfield, U.S.A. Author of Teaching for Spiritual Growth (Zondervan, 1994). As licensed foster parents, he and his wife have cared for 28 children in difficult circumstances.

Clare Hanbury. Program officer of the Child-to-Child Trust (U.K.) for English-speaking Africa, Southeast Asia, the Far East, Eastern Europe and the U.K. Qualified middle school teacher who has taught in Kenya and Hong Kong. Master's dissertation, "Education in Developing Countries," examined education programs in refugee camps. Travels extensively and is particularly interested in training and programs that assist children in difficult circumstances.

David High. Born and raised in Nigeria, West Africa, son of missionary parents. Finished undergraduate work at Furman University and received a master's degree in exercise physiology at the University of Tennessee in 1986. Received a call to be a "father to the fatherless" while visiting an orphanage in Santos, Brazil, in 1983. This call led to the founding of Homeless Children International in 1991, where he serves as president.

Phyllis Kilbourn. Ed.D. from Trinity International University. Missionary with WEC International since 1967, serving in Kenya and Liberia. Currently director of WEC's program for children in crisis, Rainbows of Hope. Editor of *Healing the Children of War: A handbook for ministry to children who have suffered deep trauma* and *Children in Crisis: A New Commitment*. Conducted research on street children in Asia, Latin America and North America.

Carole A. McKelvey. M.A. in psychology, Regis University, Denver, U.S.A. Member of the Colorado Counseling Association. Editor, author and counselor with Connell Watkins and Associates of Evergreen, Colorado. Co-author of three books: *High Risk: Children without a Conscience* (Bantam, 1988); *Adoption Crisis: The Truth About Adoption and Foster Care* (Fulcrum Books, 1994); and *Out of the Frying Pan: Foreign Adoption* (Pocket Books, 1996.

Doug Nichols. Graduate of Prairie Bible Institute. Has pastored churches, worked with the Northwest Independent Church Extension and was program director of a Christian camp with Union Gospel Mission, a Seattle inner city ministry. Served with Operation Mobilization in India, Overseas Missionary Fellowship in the Philippines and currently serves as international president for Action International Ministries.

Eric R. Ram. From India, received Ph.D. in international health from the University of North Carolina at Chapel Hill, U.S.A. Serves as the World Vision Partnership's international director for global health programs. Based in Geneva, Switzerland, where he also serves as director of the international liaison office of World Vision International. Prior to serving with World Vision, he was the director of the Christian Medical Commission of the World Council of Churches in Geneva. Also served as consultant and advisor to WHO and UNICEF. Dr. Ram has written extensively, and is editor of *Transforming Health: Christian Approaches to Healing and Wholeness*.

Helen Shedd. Graduate of Wheaton College with B.A. degrees in theology and psychology. Engaged in master level studies at the Baptist Seminary of Sao Paulo, Brazil. From 1989-91, worked with JEAME (Jesus Loves the Minor) in Sao Paulo, where she directed a pioneering project in the area of street outreach. Worked more broadly with several ministries to street children during 1992-94, serving as a resource person.

Leah Wenthe. M. A. in forensic psychology from City University of New York/John Jay College of Criminal Justice, New

York, U.S.A. From 1993 to the present, serves as coordinator of Covenant House New York, where she manages a residential crisis care program servicing runaway and homeless teen mothers and pregnant teens.

Acknowledgements

Imust express deep appreciation to each writer who assisted with this vital project. Believing that street children are worthy of their finest endeavors, they generously gave their time and expertise as a gift to the millions of children eking out a difficult and lonely existence on our cities' danger-filled streets.

The diversity of the team has fostered a unique blend of perspectives, ideas, strategies and cultural richness. The team is comprised of writers from Africa, Asia, Latin America, Europe and North America. The blend is further strengthened by the diversity of backgrounds represented by the writers: international and national mission presidents, researchers, authors, a medical doctor, field and project workers and directors, strategists and professors.

WEC International's Fort Washington residential headquarters was my launching and landing pad during the year of research and writing for this book. Thus much appreciation is due my mission family. Their prayers sustained me during times of "battle fatigue," especially through periods of extensive research travel. WEC editor Marj McDermid was always eager to brandish her magic red pen, giving my pages a healthy dose of measles. How I cherish her encouragement and counsel!

Finally, much gratitude is due MARC editors John Kenyon and Edna Valdez, who have worked hard and long on the final layout, editing and polishing of the manuscript. Their superb craftsmanship is much appreciated.

Our prayer is that this handbook will be a valuable tool to assist you in the task of reaching out to needy street children, providing them with love, holistic healing and hope for a meaningful future.

Phyllis Kilbourn

Foreword

John, Rick and I boarded the bus just before midnight in the heart of the world's third largest city—Sao Paulo, Brazil. We were accompanied by Pastor Nonato and Carlao, a converted street kid. These two regularly work the streets in an effort to bring more of these "kids" to the Savior and out of the bondage of their sordid life of drugs, sex and thievery. With us that night was young Marcello, who had been at camp but would not return to his abusive home. He kept running away, traveling for hours on Sao Paulo's complex transit system. He spent many nights on the street, but most loved to be with John, whom he trusted. His head fell to John's shoulder as he drifted off to sleep. He was eleven years old.

In many countries around the world, missionaries continue to give shoulders, hands, hearts and words to children desperately in need of the love and security that comes from the arms of the Good Shepherd. Can you remember how loving hands touched you as a child:

- the gentle stroking of a fevered brow;
- the careful bandaging of scrapes and bruises;
- the steady hand on your shoulder as you wobbled your way toward a bike-rider's freedom;
- the tickles;
- the hand-in-hand in a bustling crowd;
- the tender hugs and "night-nights" at bedtime?

These "touches" were the expressions of a family and a society that cared for its children.

Now let's think of another childhood and the "hands" that must have touched it. This childhood—if we can call it that—ended several years ago on the main street of Ipanema, Brazil. The body of nine-year-old Patricio Hilario da Silva was found with a handwritten note tied around his neck. It read, "I killed you because you didn't study and had no future. The government must not allow the streets of the city to be invaded by kids."

In the world today, possibly 100 million children make their homes on the street. In Brazil alone, conservative estimates indicate probably 10 million children like Patricio "living" on the streets. That would be equivalent to every kindergarten through eighth grade child in the states of California, Illinois, New York and Texas . . . out on the streets!

The world's most precious resource is being thrown out into the street, considered "vermin" and "garbage." Documented evidence shows that merchants, hired mercenaries and even police, in countries like Brazil, are methodically attacking, torturing and even killing children they find on the streets. "Cleaning up the cities" has taken on an unthinkably twisted meaning.

The vast majority, however, do not end up like Patricio. Left to themselves, they die the much slower deaths of prostitution, drug abuse (primarily glue-sniffing), petty crime, sickness, chronic malnutrition and street violence. Some are as young as seven years old. Girls are often prostitutes by the age of ten.

The hands that have touched these children have not gently stroked, guided, tickled or protected. They have, at best, been powerless or indifferent; at worst, they have been deadly.

Today's Christian workers among street children cannot turn a situation like this around, but they can give their shoulders, hands, hearts and words to little lost sheep and make an eternal difference to a potential Marcello or Patricio, and many more like them. The one who said, "Let the little ones come unto me," and who placed his hands upon them and blessed them, is commanding us to act. He is asking more of us to be God's hands that reach out to provide that loving compassionate touch.

In today's world of desperate poverty and family dysfunction, concerned parents are rare and the government has all but given up. Christians must mobilize and provide strategic intervention in neighborhoods, parks, streets and centers so that these "little ones" are rescued from the violent, exploitative, evil society around them. It is not an easy task, as chapters in this book will demonstrate, but respond we must. To our Lord Jesus, such children are not trash—they are treasures!

Larry W. Sharp
UFM International

PART ONE:

Street Children and Street Life

1

Street Children:
Who are they? Where are they?

Phyllis Kilbourn

Street children. How does one describe these millions of children who make the streets their home and source of livelihood? Children who are abandoned and battered by family and society, growing up knowing little about love, kindness, justice or security. Children having a "legacy of abandonment spelled out in such words as rootless, worthless and homeless."[1] Children who must fight every day just to find enough food to survive and who constantly are on the move in search of shelter, often finding none.

The answer to this multifaceted question depends on to whom you direct the question. The children themselves, their parents, local citizens and the law all have descriptive name tags for these children.

Dagala, a thirteen-year-old street child who lost his parents, siblings and home in the Ugandan civil war, considers himself an *orphan*. Lakshmi, who ran away from a violent and abusive home situation when she was fifteen, calls herself *abused and unloved*. Asha, who was sold to a pimp by her mother and now finds herself living in a lewd, filthy brothel,

7

portrays herself as not only *abandoned,* but also irretrievably *polluted.*

When Juan's father was put in jail, Juan's mother pushed him and his two younger siblings out of their home, telling them to never return. Selling pencils in San Jose to support himself and his siblings, Juan feels they have become *disowned, castoffs.* Roberto's mother, living in poverty in the bustling city of Sao Paulo, claims that Roberto is *just another mouth to feed* and prefers he fend for himself.

Mary's mother and father, both drug addicts and selling drugs in New York's underworld, constantly reminded Mary that she was *an unwanted burden* that interfered with their lifestyle. When her parents eventually died of AIDS, Mary decided to live life on her own, not wanting to become someone else's unwanted burden. Rosanna, whose mother is single, jobless and an alcoholic, has heard her mother repeatedly call her *an unexpected accident,* along with such name tags as *a headache or an added expense.* Feeling the lack of love and acceptance from her mother, and knowing she is not wanted, Mary has chosen to become yet another child who makes the streets her home.

Local citizens who see children like Mary, Juan and his siblings or Roberto huddled in alleyways or on park benches throw the words *nuisance* or *good-for-nothing kids* at them. Children like Mary, who already have experienced so much rejection in life, feel an immense sting in such words. Shopkeepers who catch Juan snatching fruit for himself and his younger siblings label him a *thief* or *criminal.* But Juan wonders what else he can do to provide food for them when there is no drop-in center in his neighborhood or available work.

In Manila Rosanna, who has taken to glue-sniffing as a respite from the cold, hunger and loneliness of street life, is described as *trash.* Asha finds life as a prostitute both repulsive and dangerous, yet she has no way of eluding the pimp to whom her mother sold her. Just as frightening are the slim prospects of finding another way to earn a living if she did run away from him. Knowing she is thought of as one of many *disposable ones* on the streets of Colombia—unloved, despised and a troublesome problem to be eliminated at all costs—does not

Street children sleeping on the sidewalk in Harare, Zimbabwe.

give her hope for her future. But, she reflects, I didn't choose to live this way.

Dagala joined a street gang to take the place of the family he lost in war. Gang members are precious to him, providing comfort, identity and a sense of belonging. The police, not liking the gang's presence and activities, call them *nasty kids*. Roberto, already tagged as another mouth to feed, discovers that to the police he is considered *vermin, garbage* or *a blight on society*. All he can conclude is that his life is all screwed up—nobody wants him, he has no hope that things will get better.

The "law" provides even more graphic descriptions for children like Rosanna, Asha, Roberto and Dagala. Police in Brazil think they are doing society a favor by getting rid of these children through such activities as police sweeps. They are quick to point out that if the children are allowed to grow up, they will be nothing more than criminals. So the police even "moonlight" by contracting to kill them. Thousands of children have been killed in the past year alone.

Every society has its own way of describing children of the street; these name tags speak volumes about the lack of respect, value and dignity societies hold for their children. As concerned caregivers, we cannot allow these name tags to stick—tags that not only humiliate precious children who have been created in the image of God, but that give credence to the unfair and total exploitation of their precious young lives.

To effectively offer hope to these children, caregivers must sense and value other vital descriptive name tags for them: the heroic child, the lonely child, the unprotected child, the "hungry-for-love" child, the child of inestimable value, the resilient child, the child deeply cherished by his or her Creator God.

Who are they?

The meanings given to "street children" vary widely across countries and cultures. The term generally refers to children who live or spend a significant amount of time on the streets of urban areas to fend for themselves or their families; this also denotes children who are inadequately protected, supervised and cared for by responsible adults.

The purpose of this book is to target the needs of *all* street children. For effective intervention planning, however, it is important to be aware of the various groups that the term "street children" embraces:

1. Children *on* the street, or children with regular family contact. Most of these children work on the streets because their families need money to survive. Many of them go to school and return home to their families at the end of the day.

   Besides working, some children are on the streets to have fun, to pass time or to escape the overcrowded conditions in their homes. Also in this group are children from squatter families and the slums. These children have nothing to do in their homes so they frequently roam the streets, returning home only at night or at mealtime.

   This group of children, not yet deeply entrenched in street life, are more easily reached. They especially need to be targeted by prevention programs.

2. Children *of* the street, or children with occasional family contact. These children work on the street, do not go to school and seldom go home to their families.

   This group includes children from poverty-stricken families. Some have come to the city from deprived rural areas; others are runaways. Many run away from home because of sexual and physical abuse, parental alcoholism and neglect or mistreatment by relatives. Home has become a place of fear and misery rather than security, love and encouragement.

   These children, if they are to survive, are faced with the need to find food and shelter daily. They also need to find a sense of identity and belonging among peers. Soon the children come to enjoy their newly-found independence, free of adult control. It is vital to get the children in this group off the street before they become addicted to street life.

3. Children *in* the street, or children with no family contact. These children consider the streets their home. Here they seek shelter, food and a sense of belonging among peers.

   This group represents children who are detached from their families and are either living on the streets or in shelters.

11

Some are orphans whose parents have been killed in war or have died from illnesses such as AIDS. Others have been abandoned by parents who were unable to care for them.

These children are not only victims of physical isolation but are also alone psychologically. In some cases these children have no memory of what home life was like. Working with this group of children is the most difficult. Because they have been badly abused by adults they should have been able to trust, winning their confidence is very difficult.

Where are they?

Geographically, you will find street children in almost every major city all over the world. Whenever a devastating social, political or economic crisis or upheaval occurs such as famine, drought or civil war, people converge en masse to the cities to seek food and refuge. Mass movements to the world's cities result in extreme poverty for millions, increasing family disintegration and causing an unprecedented rise in the number of street children.[2]

The casual passerby will find it difficult to locate children living on the streets. For their own protection, the children usually do not choose to spread their newspapers and sleep in open places. Instead, they seek safety and a place where they can be left alone for a few hours in all sorts of unusual and dangerous "street abodes": in cardboard boxes tucked away in dark and dangerous alleyways, inside the cities' subway systems or under bridges, in abandoned railroad cars or on benches in vacated city parks.

Adrian Croft[3] describes how Jaime Jaramillo, a successful geophysical consultant in the oil industry, goes in search of homeless children who take shelter in the dark, dismal nooks and crannies of Bogota's sewerage system. Here they can avoid the police and escape possible death from "clean-up squads"—vigilantes who hunt down the children as if they were criminals. Jaramillo was introduced to the world of the sewers by a homeless girl he had helped.

After midnight, Jaramillo leaves his comfortable apartment, puts on scuba gear and descends into the sewers beneath

Colombia's sprawling capital where many children make their home. Without the scuba gear Jaramillo, like so many of the children, could drown or be swept away in the torrents after a storm. The breathing apparatus also helps to avoid the stench from the sewers.

Oscar is one of many street children found by Jaramillo. Oscar had lived in the city sewers for six years, claiming that it was better than living exposed on the surface. He scratched out a living by scavenging for cardboard, which he sold. Oscar now has an exciting new beginning working in Jaramillo's oil fields.

How many?

It is extremely difficult to count the number of street children as they move around during the day and hide when they sleep. Their number also depends on the criteria chosen in defining them and the age groupings used. United Nations estimates put the number of children living on the streets of the world's cities at 100 million; other estimates are closer to 200 million. The amount is increasing and some street educators and researchers believe it could double within a generation unless effective action is taken.

To help us grasp the reality of how many children are living on the streets, various comparisons have been made: Twice as many street children in Latin America as there are people in Canada; or more street children globally than the populations of France and Britain combined.

Distressing trends

There appear to be increasing numbers of younger and younger children reduced to street-living. Some nations are even beginning to see children of street children being born directly into the street—children who will know no other home than the street.

Most street children in poorer countries are boys; poverty often drives them onto the streets. In developed nations, the majority of runaway homeless young people are girls. In Western and Third World countries, sexual abuse is a chief reason why girls turn to a life on the street.

Boys from families in the slums are expected to provide enough money to look after themselves before they are teens.

13

A street child trying to survive on the streets of Bucharest, Romania.

Some have to earn enough to cover the cost of living at home. While other youths have their minds on soccer games and other sports, music, movies or the latest fads in clothes, these children have neither time, money or energy for such diversions. Survival dominates their thoughts and actions.

As they become used to life on the streets, many children decide not to return home. The youngest at which a child can contribute to family income or survive in a street gang is thought to be about age five. More commonly, boys start their street existence around the age of seven or eight and peak at about fifteen.

Poverty also forces some parents to abandon one or more of their children to street life in the hope that their other children will survive. Sometimes children themselves want to leave the poor sanitation, cramped living conditions and hunger of their neighborhood. They hope for a better life on the streets.

In a number of countries children are on the streets and separated from their families through direct exploitation such as slavery, bonded labor (to pay off their parents' or grandparents' debt), forced prostitution or sold for payment for something as little as a new television set.

Survival tactics

Street children, like Dagala mentioned earlier, join gangs for survival and to learn how to become street-wise. Membership in a gang provides a child with comfort and support from other children with whom they can identify. The gangs also function as surrogate families, providing children with a sense of identity, of belonging and protection. They become family to one another, together fending off the brutality and difficulties of life as best they can. These gangs typically are composed of older and younger children. Members exhibit fierce loyalty to their gang, standing faithfully by one another in times of sickness, when beaten or when arrested and put in prison.

The World Health Organization[4] (WHO) points out that while the streets and their occupants provide the children with a sense of belonging to a new and often more caring replacement "family," there is a price to pay. This price may be a near total absence of privacy, supervision, education, nurturing and security, and the likelihood of hunger, violence, marginal employment and exploitation.

The street children's frightening, abusive and violence-filled environment, along with their deep sense of hopelessness, provides a vivid expression of the misery and social alienation they experience. In light of these high-risk situations, we must also recognize the remarkable degree of resiliency demonstrated by the children. They face situations that would prove too daunting for most adults. Christopher Lowry[5] points out that, "Street children are survivors. Every day they confront challenges and suffer indignities that most of us could not endure."

What does the future hold?

All children have dreams, goals and things they value: friends, the opportunity to attend school and have an adequate education, food, shelter, medical care, physical and emotional safety, acceptance and self-esteem. Children from loving, nurturing families have hopes of realizing such goals and desires. But the realities of street life force children to drastically alter or forever erase their childhood hopes, dreams and lifestyles— even their most simple desires.

Peter Tacon,[6] veteran children's worker, asked Latin American street children what was the biggest wish of their entire lives. Their dreams went as follows:

♦ Ramon drooled over a vivid description of a sumptuous dinner;

♦ Ten-year-old Lelia pleaded for the chance to go to school—she longed to be able to read and write;

♦ Jorge simply pointed to his tattered clothes and bare feet, saying nothing;

♦ Ricardo looked up from his shoe shine box to whisper wearily that what he has always wanted in his 12 years is a father;

♦ Marta's aggressive retort was, "To be left alone!" Hers was a poignant testimony to the abuse and violence she had experienced;

♦ Twins Arturo and Antonio repeated over and over their desire to have their young lost mother with them again;

♦ Street-wise Gato, 13, betrayed his normally arrogant air by letting slip his secret longing for a real home, a joy he has never known;

♦ After thoughtful reflection, 9-year-old Benji stated firmly that his greatest wish in all of life would be to work.

This "wish list" is far different from what we would expect from children in affluent Western countries. The requests of Western children might range from a pair of designer jeans or the latest style of athletic shoes, to the newest music CD, computer game or scuba diving gear. The Latin American children's wishes, however, were for things that most of us take for granted: a home, good food, a family, school, the chance to play and work, the freedom from fear of violence.

In most societies, these children constitute a marginalized group. Accessibility to basic health care and other services are severely restricted. Their living situations make the children vulnerable to sexual exploitation and drug abuse, which lead to other severe problems, adding to the overall burdens of their lives. Street children are forced to live without a childhood, forced to grow up and assume adult responsibilities at a very young age. They grow up apart from the two most important institutions of socialization that provide guidance and structure for children's development: the family and the school.

They face insults, beatings, stabbings, accidents and assaults on the violent streets where they live. Only the hardened survive. Perhaps a "survival mentality" best describes their social, psychological and spiritual situations. Mac Margolis,[7] talking about the street children in Rio de Janeiro, says that, "Deep down the kids plainly don't want to be on the street. Yet very few seem capable of escaping, even when given the opportunity."

We must make a difference

Street children have lost their way in life, their values and their sense of worth as individuals who have been created in the image of God. Their purpose as valuable members of families, communities and societies has been obliterated.

James Grant, the late executive director of UNICEF, stated at the second International Encounter of Street Children in Rio de Janeiro, Brazil, that it was "personally unacceptable, ethically unthinkable, that on the eve of the twenty-first century children and youth by the tens of millions should have to call the streets their homes."

My deep desire is that the body of Christ will come to that same conclusion. And further, that Christians will prove the sincerity of their convictions by offering hope to these children who so desperately need a hope to cling to, a hope that bestows on them a deep sense of purpose, worth and dignity.

As Jeff Anderson powerfully warns us, "Only our heavenly Father knows how he will use one of these street children after he redeems them from the 'trash heap.'"[8] Yes, to society

17

these children may appear to be only troublemakers, nuisances or an embarrassing blight on society, but to their Creator who commanded, "Let the little children come to me," they are precious jewels. For churches, families and societies they are a bundle of gifts and potential with which God has blessed us. May we find abundant joy in facilitating the restoration of these precious lives to God-ordained purposes.

NOTES

1   John R. Cheyne, "Street Children: A New Frontier," in *The Commission* (April 1993), p. 82.

2   Jo Boyden, *Children of the Cities* (London: Zed Books, 1991).

3   Adrian Croft for Reuters in Colombia, "Sewer Diving for the Urchins of Colombia," in *Detroit Times* (25 April 1990).

4   *Program on Substance Abuse: Report on Phase 1 of the Street Children Project*, World Health Organization, 1993, p. 7.

5   Christopher Lowry, "Development Communication Report," in *Street Kids International*, No. 81, p. 12.

6   From *A Child's Biggest Wish*, a leaflet published by Action International Ministries, Manila, Philippines.

7   Mac Margolis, "Children of the Gutter," in *Newsweek* (May 1, 1989), p. 184.

8   Jeff Anderson, *Manila Heartbeat*, Vol. 10, No. 2, 2nd quarter 1994, p. 1.

2

Why are children on the streets?

Tony Culnane

Life's aspirations come in the guise of children.
—Rabindranath Tagore

And they were bringing children to him [Jesus], that he might
touch them; and the disciples rebuked them. But when Jesus saw
it he was indignant, and said to them, "Let the children come to
me, do not hinder them; for to such belongs the kingdom of God"
(Mark 10:13-14).

The opening quotation and Jesus' angry response to his disciples point to two universal truths. First, children represent hope for the future of humankind in this world. Second, they embody the establishment of the kingdom of God as a present reality and as a vision of humankind's ultimate destiny.

When I ponder these ideas, the word "childlike" comes to mind. Initially I think about smiling, laughing, playing, happiness, joy, innocence, frankness, dependence. I feel encouraged and thankful as I reflect on my own happy memories of childhood. I am also grateful for the many positive experiences I have had with children.

A global problem

When confronted with the statistic of 100 million children living and working on the streets—40 million in Latin America, 25 million in Asia, 10 million in Africa, the 25 million living on the streets of Western cities—my thoughts are quite different.

I feel sad and frustrated. I think about crying, pain, grief, exploitation, bewilderment, hopelessness, deceit and greed. The word "monstrous" comes to mind. Then I know with certainty that life's aspirations are not represented in street children nor is the kingdom of God embodied in their lives. These thoughts lead me to ask, "Why are children on the streets?"

An urban problem

Until three years ago, life in the countryside for Srey and her brothers was good. But the last three rice-planting seasons had been poor. They either had too much or too little rain. Three years of crop failure had put the family so deeply in debt they were forced to leave their land. Like Srey, many others were faced with the same situation. They felt their best move would be to the city.

They envisaged that work would be easier to obtain in the city. That, however, has not been the case. Having no money, the children cannot attend school. They are forced to join their parents on the streets, scrounging the rubbish heaps for items to sell. They also beg for money.

Almost everywhere, observations by aid workers confirm the increase in the number of street children and its exclusively urban nature; there are no rural street children. This increase is due to rapid urbanization and massive population displacement throughout the world, particularly in the developing world. Around one and a half billion people in developing countries live in cities. This figure is expected to double in the next twenty years.

In the 1950s, by contrast, fewer than 300 million people in the Third World were city dwellers. The world has never before encountered such rapid urbanization on so massive a scale. As Messignon points out, "It brings with it the danger of disequilibrium and strain because the demands to be met are huge. Further the policies, infrastructure and services to cope with them are not yet in place."[1]

The reality is that more and more people are falling into poverty. Once prevalent in rural areas, poverty now is primarily an urban problem. The World Bank states bluntly that poverty in urban areas could become one of the most explosive political problems of the twenty-first century.[2]

Victims of poverty

> *A family of four children was living with an elderly grand-mother. Both parents were dead. The eldest child was a boy of 14. The grandmother was elderly, frail and unable to work. A researcher visiting the home found they were unable to afford meat or fish. Eating only rice porridge with salt, they were malnourished. There were holes in the roof of their house. The four-teen-year-old boy was forced to spend most of his time roaming the streets, begging for money.*

The most obvious manifestation of poverty is the presence of numerous street children. Field workers observe that while genuine street children may be rare in the cities of the developed world, street youngsters or runaway youth are far from rare. Most of the street children in industrial countries are victims of inner city decay. This results in inadequate housing and job markets, family break-ups, high divorce rates and one-parent families. These factors cause deprivation and places great stress on individuals and families.

James Grant, the late executive director of UNICEF, recognized that family disintegration is a major cause of children being on the street. But he also emphasized that there are other forces at work, "a chain of events" that can force a child onto the street, including models of development that simply do not work for entire sectors of the population. Grant also blamed an urbanization process that has shattered traditional structures, an increasingly degraded and unlivable natural environment and inadequate or nonexistent social safety nets. Lines of causality, he believed, could even be drawn connecting the street child to an international economic system that has accelerated impoverishment and stalled development in much of the Third World.[3]

Bruce McConchie, vice president of partnership coordination for World Vision International, describes poverty as the absence of choice, a truism applying to all countries. The poor

STREET CHILDREN

Figure 2.1. The Consequences Tree and Root Causes[4]

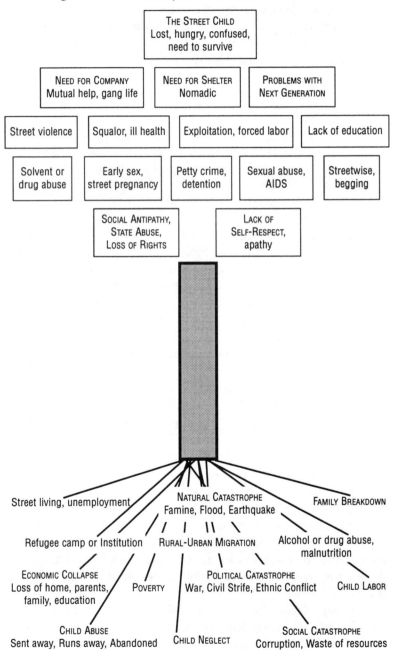

everywhere have limited choices. The effect is especially notice-able when it comes to such basic needs as food, shelter, health care, education, water and sanitation. Wherever the poor live, the causes of their poverty are surprisingly similar. They have poor education, limited access to resources, and encounter injustice from economic, social and political systems. To experi-ence poverty, whether in the north or the south, means facing similar issues; only the relative impact changes.[5]

A 1991 survey on street children in Namibia resulted in a composite portrait of a typical Namibian street child. This typ-ical child is male, black, poor and between 11 and 14 years old. His family also is poor. He goes home regularly, if not nightly. He likely has a mother who heads his family and who usually is unemployed. He has four to seven siblings, making a total family group of six to nine members who live with four or six more family members in the same house. He works on the street to earn food or money to support his family. His family is involved in alcohol or substance abuse. If he attends school, he usually drops out after one or two years. He is physically or psychologically abused at home but still has some self-esteem and a desire to be esteemed and respected by others. He is eager to learn and anxious to improve his lot in life.[6] Other sur-veys in Africa also have confirmed this general profile.

Delia Paul, a researcher with World Vision Australia, notes that poverty is a complex phenomenon comprising many special and psychological factors besides economic ones. When I worked at the World Vision Centre in Cambodia, many of the children there were not from the most destitute of families. Rather, their poverty had to do with the limited ability of par-ents or adults to provide an atmosphere of security for the child. It was clear from the case notes and interviews that staff conducted that many children had been in the care of adults facing extreme stresses themselves.[7]

Poverty and natural and human-made disasters

The face of the earth is constantly being reshaped by nature's forces and by the actions of humans. All areas of the world are subject to these processes, which cause loss of life and poverty. They also have deleterious effects on social and eco-nomic development. Millions of people are affected by natural

23

disasters, and at least 250,000 die as a direct result of these disasters every year.

The number of disaster victims in developing countries is disproportionately high. The World Bank estimates that 95 percent of disaster-related deaths occur among the 66 percent of the world's population that live in poorer countries. Disasters such as occurred at Bhopal and Chernobyl are but two of the more dramatic human-made disasters in recent years. The consequences of these will be felt for decades to come.[8]

The social consequences of disasters are even less apparent. We can quantify some immediate consequences, such as people left homeless by disaster. The 1990 Luzon earthquake in the Philippines left 120,000 people homeless. Some one million houses were destroyed by storms and floods in Vietnam in the 1980s and another three million houses were damaged. It is known that the poor suffer disproportionately from these disasters.

The poor depend on family networks for mutual assistance and support in times of hardship. Disasters further strain these networks. Ignasio Armillas states, "This, exacerbated by economic hardships, often creates a second set of disaster victims—those who survived the event physically unharmed but are nonetheless affected by the consequences."[9]

Families and individual children affected by disasters have few choices. Often moving to the city and living on the street becomes their way of life.

Victims of the crisis of the family

Purity is one of six children. His father used to sell drugs. When his father was arrested, the family's situation was desperate. His mother tried washing clothes to support the children. Purity was too embarrassed to go to school; he had no clothes. His community is a tough and dangerous place. Until his family was able to receive assistance, Purity was forced to roam the streets with other children, struggling to find ways to make some money.

A study of street children in Asia concludes that the breakdown of traditional family life and community values and structures are major factors in the increase of children on the streets.[10] Parents could depend on extended families or neighborhood groups to come to their aid when they could not adequately care for their children. In the urban jungle, where survival is the name of the game, this tradition seems to have weakened considerably.

Parents who cannot take the strain of supporting their families frequently end up fighting. The men turn to drinking or to other vices and finally the family breaks up. Such family disunity all too frequently causes parents to vent their anger or frustration on their children through physical or emotional abuse. Faced with deprivation, neglect and sometimes brutality in their homes, these children view the streets as a better alternative.

War and armed conflict: Destroyers of family life

> *Sok was a normal, fun-loving thirteen-year-old living on the edge of a war zone. She was out tending the cattle with her friends, just as she had done almost every other day. But this day she took a different path and stepped on something. It clicked and the next thing she remembered was that she was lying in a pool of blood and couldn't move. Then she realized her leg was missing. Sok is now 18 and walks with the help of crutches. Her friends are all married now, and she worries about her future. Her chances of marriage are very slim. Men won't even consider marrying a disabled woman. Marriage and motherhood are highly valued in her society and she believes her dreams of family will not be fulfilled.*

An increasing "feminization of poverty" is a cause for particular concern. Armed conflicts and civil disturbances in many countries have displaced increasing numbers of women and children. Such women become the heads of their households with few resources to provide for their families' basic needs and limited opportunities to improve their situation. Many such families move from their devastated rural homes to urban centers. Many of the children in these families become street children.

According to UNICEF, in the past ten years armed conflict has uprooted some 12 million children from their communities. At least five million more have become refugees. More than one million have been orphaned or separated from their parents by war and armed conflict. Grinding poverty and extraordinary dangers dominate the lives of children affected by war and armed conflict. Yet loss of home and family is their greatest fear.

Up to 5 percent of a refugee population consists of unac-
companied children who have become lost, separated or
orphaned in the panic of flight from armed conflict. At the end
of 1994 in Rwanda, an estimated 114,000 children had been separated from their families.

In more and more countries, the steady drift to the urban
centers is, to a large extent, a consequence of the disruption to
settled rural life by war and armed conflict. Furthermore, land-
mines kill and maim thousands and make access to formerly
arable land a lottery, a Russian roulette game of chance. War in
all its forms causes the destruction of traditional family life.
Those affected experience true poverty; they have limited
choices. Often the street becomes their life.

All are victims of family crisis

According to Susanna Agnelli, wherever children are on
the street they can be described as victims of the crisis of the
family. Agnelli points out that the breakdowns of family structure and traditional values, and mass emigrations to cities in
economic decline provide many similarities in day-to-day living and problem solving for children everywhere.[11]

Children and sexual exploitation

*Roberto is 15 and has been a street child for two years. He ran
away from his village home after enduring two years of beatings
by his stepfather. One day a foreign man stopped and talked with
Roberto on the street. He seemed kind and interested in
Roberto's life and told him he would help him by sending him to
school. He asked Roberto to meet him later that night. After
meeting, he took Roberto to a guest house where he gave him a
nice T-shirt and some biscuits.*

*Soon he asked Roberto to bathe with him in the bath. Roberto
was very uneasy, but the man said he would give him $2.00 to
wash his whole body very carefully. Roberto did so and then
quickly took the money and left the guest house. This was the
most money Roberto had made in such a short time. He was
tempted to return. The next time, however, the foreigner forced
him to submit to anal intercourse that was very painful and
humiliating. Again, he was paid $2.00 and invited to come back.
Roberto is very confused. He does not know what to do.*

Each year more than one million children worldwide are

reportedly forced into child prostitution, trafficked and sold for sexual purposes or used in child pornography. Coerced or lured into the world's sex market—a multi-billion dollar industry—children are denied their rights, their dignity and their childhood. Commercial sexual exploitation subjects children to one of the most hazardous forms of child labor, endangers their mental and physical health and undermines all aspects of their development. This inhuman growth industry exists in virtually every country in the world. Cross-border trafficking and kidnaping of children from rural villages to sell in major cities are common occurrences.

Most of these children are girls, but there are many reports that a growing number of boys are becoming involved; most of them are between the ages of 14-18 years. There is, however, mounting information of a greater demand for even younger children due to the customers' fear of AIDS and sexually transmitted diseases. Many of these children are deceived, kidnaped or sold by their parents or relatives. Others have run away from abuse and neglect at home. Some have become prostitutes to survive and to improve their lives

Often sexually exploited children end up on the streets when they are abandoned by the brothel owners. Usually these children are sick and even dying from sexually transmitted diseases, including AIDS. Some return to their home villages but they rarely stay. Often they are rejected by family, friends and their village when news gets out concerning what they had been involved in while in the city.

In the U.S.A., field workers estimate that there are 300,000 child prostitutes, male and female, under the age of 16. Most of these children have escaped neglect or abuse by their parents, only to be exploited by other adults. In Britain each year more than 7,000 children are so badly hurt by their parents that they need medical treatment.[12] In Australia, according to the Human Rights Commission, some 500,000 children are homeless and over 20,000 children cannot live with their own families because of emotional, physical and sexual abuse and neglect.[13]

Ron O'Grady notes there is no evidence that children who have been systematically prostituted for more than a short time can ever be successfully rehabilitated. He says that when a child is being forced to have several sexual partners seven nights a week, the traumatic effect appears to be impossible to overcome. The experience of social workers in Asia is that very few children rescued from brothels have been able to begin living a healthy life, emotionally or physically.[14]

Street children's interpretation of the problem

> Jessie lived with her mother and father. Jessie, like all rural children, was expected to do chores to help the family. One chore was to walk a distance to fetch water. One day, having lots to do, she hastened to get her work done before dark. Just as she got home, she slipped and spilled the water. Her mother, also tired from working so hard, picked up an axe and hit her daughter on the head. Jessie was so frightened she ran away from home. She made her way to the capital where she lived on the streets, begging and stealing. The crowd of people surrounding her noticed her. She was taken to a hospital where she was diagnosed as epileptic, probably as a result from the blow on the head. Jessie now has a deep dent in her skull and has to take medication every day to control the epilepsy.

Children give many reasons for being on the street. Eric Ram reports that most children living on city streets claim breakdowns in their family structure, poverty, physical or sexual abuse, parental exploitation, armed conflicts and war, natural and human-caused disasters, famine, dislocation through migration and substance abuse by parents as some of the reasons for living on the streets.[15]

Cornelio Bansang, a psychiatrist in Manila, provides a similar perspective from his work with street children. He has found many of these children come from large families that are disorganized and not well supervised by adults. Parents are often engrossed in their own problems and are slow to provide care and protection for their children. When children get sick, they are often not taken to a healer; many of their basic needs are unmet. The children then become restless and go out into the streets to look for something that will make them happy. They enjoy freedom in the streets and become disengaged from their families. To cope, many develop antisocial behavior.[16]

Reflection

Mahatma Gandhi observed that if we are to make true peace in the world, we must begin with the children. The preamble to the United Nations charter includes these words: "Mankind owes to the child the very best it can give."

These two challenges coincide. They confront us all and beg the question, "Why are they on the streets?"

NOTES

1   Nicole Messignon, "The Urban Explosion in the Third World," in *The OECD Observer* (No. 182, June-July 1993).

2   Ibid.

3   James Grant, *Esperanza* (Vol. 5, Winter/Spring 1993), Childhope Asia.

4   Adapted from "The Consequences Tree and Root Causes," text by UK Consortium for Street Children, Art by Our Local Economy, Toronto, Canada. Used by permission.

5   Bruce McConchie, "Facing Poverty, North or South," in *Together* (July-September 1992).

6   Jean-Pierre Velis, "Blossoms in the Dust: Street Children in Africa," in *Youth Plus* (1995), UNESCO Publishing.

7   Delia Paul, "Street Survival: Children, Work and Urban Drift in Cambodia," in *Issues in Global Development* (No. 3, July 1995), World Vision Australia.

8   Ignasio Armillas, "Acts of Nature, Acts of Men," in *Habitat Debate* (Vol. 1, No. 2, August 1995).

9   Ibid.

10 Childhope Asia, "Causes of the Street Children Phenomenon," in *The Street Children of Asia: A Profile* (1993).

11 Susanna Agnelli, "Street Children: A Growing Urban Tragedy," in a report for the Independent Commission on International Humanitarian Issues (1986), Weidenfeld and Nicolson.

12 Graeme Irvine, "Abandoned Children: The Most Marginalized," in *Together* (October-December 1991).

13 "Sharing our Future." *Report of the Australia Association of Young People in Care* (1995).

14 Ron O'Grady, "Ending the Prostitution of Asian Children," an address to the Tenth International Congress on Prevention of Child Abuse and Neglect. Kuala Lumpur, Malaysia, September 1994.

15 Eric Ram, "Health Risks Faced by Street Children," in *Together* (October-December 1994).

16 Cornelio Bansang, "The Psycho-Dynamics of the Behavior of Street Children." A report presented during the proceedings of the Cambodian Field Study Visit and Program Development Workshop (April 1993), Manila, Philippines. Childhope Asia in cooperation with UNICEF Cambodia.

3

Surviving on the streets

Alemtsehai Alemu

Rio de Janeiro—The killers had warned the boys not to
sleep in the street. But there was nowhere else to go. "They
said they'd come back and get us," said a gangly street kid
of about 13. Seven of his companions, aged about 8 to 12,
were murdered July 23 with gunshots in the head. A sur-
vivor said a state police officer was among the killers. The
murder or "disappearance" of street kids is nothing new
in Rio, where poverty and neglect leave thousands homeless and roaming. Amnesty International issued a report
last October denouncing the torture, murder, or disappearance of thousands of poor children in Brazil's big
cities by death squads composed of, or run by, police. The
human rights group said the squads are "hired by local
shopkeepers to remove alleged criminals and petty
thieves from the area." A 1992 Brazilian congressional
investigation found that more than 4,600 street children
had been killed in the previous three years. This year, 320
have been killed in Rio alone, according to the juvenile
court.

—The Associated Press, July 24, 1993

Millions of children and adolescents work and live on the streets of the world's cities. They live in a hostile environment where every situation contains a threat to their safety and well-being. Nothing can be taken for granted; nothing is entirely safe. Every encounter with an adult, the police or another youth carries the risk of violence or exploitation. Day and night the children confront terror, violence and a deep sense of hopelessness.

The rapidly increasing number of children working and living on the streets of Ethiopia is similar to any city. Although it is difficult to get an accurate figure, as many as 100,000 Ethiopian children are estimated to be working or living on the streets.[1] Different surveys reveal that many of these children come from very poor families in the city, often from female-headed households. As the economy dwindles, many more of Ethiopia's at-risk children will swell the ranks of those seeking to eke out a living on dangerous city streets without parental nurture or guidance.

Work and survival

Survival is priority number one with the children, and survival means work. Even street children who live mostly by theft consider themselves legitimate "workers." Some children whose parents were killed in the civil war have not only themselves but siblings to support. For most of the children, life is a hard, unending drudgery with very little meaningful return. They, however, are willing to do whatever it takes to support themselves or to help their families.

By creatively using their wits, the children manage to stay alive through scrounging, foraging in garbage heaps and bartering everything from chewing gum to their own bodies. According to the children they spend most of their earnings on food. Those who have families give part of their earnings to cover family expenses. Schooling and entertainment are viewed as unaffordable luxuries.

The children are incredibly resourceful in finding or creating jobs. The boys find work as shoe shiners, peddlers selling various items like cigarettes and chewing gum, car washers or carriers of goods. Girls, especially the younger ones, sell food items like bread and peanuts. Often they have no choice of jobs or who they work for; they must accept any task that enables them to survive.

Shopkeepers and market stall owners view these industrious children as a threat and menace. They become irate at the children's nimble tactics to "make a steal," snatching fruit or vegetables from the first unwary shopkeeper or market stall vendor they spot. Businessmen not only are angry over loss of profits but also find this thieving a distraction to their own customers. As a result, many shopkeepers and market stall owners either support or participate in the brutal sweeps to rid the streets of these children.

In Ethiopia the authorities discourage the children from working on the streets. Due to the large influx of people into the capital city in the last few years, the number of adults and children working on the streets has been expanding rapidly, causing many problems such as the blocking of roads.

When there is no work for the children, or the children feel the working conditions are too difficult, they turn to begging and stealing. Many girls are attracted to prostitution as a means of earning an income which is much higher than what they would receive selling small items.

Hours of work and income

A joint survey by Ethiopia's Ministry of Labor and Social Affairs and UNICEF reported that 70 percent of the children (out of a total of 894) stated that they worked from half a day to a full day. Their income ranged from 0-4 birr per day (1 birr = 16 U.S. cents).[2] One birr is just enough to eat one meal—albeit a meal lacking in proper nutrition. Lack of proper nutrition often leaves the children hungry and tired.

Everywhere children are vulnerable to exploitation as a cheap, "expendable" form of labor. Often the child's health and general welfare are not considered in the assigning of tasks. Because children need work so desperately, and there is no one to be a voice against their exploitation, there is little the children can do to change their situations.

Dangers of working the streets

A multitude of dangers constantly lurk on city streets, ready to haunt and attack the children physically and emotionally. James Grant, the late executive director of UNICEF, spoke with street children in Rio de Janeiro. They told him that they live in "constant fear of being rejected, robbed, beaten, sexually abused, even murdered."[3]

Abuse

Street children communicate that they are physically and sexually abused on the streets. Part of the abuse is related to their work; part of it stems from life on the streets. In the Philippines Philip, a twelve-year-old, finds the streets a "lousy place to grow up." Daily he lives with fear of abuse. He is afraid of the shouting policeman. He is afraid of the older street boys and drug addicts who rob and beat him. He is very afraid of the man with the Walkman radio. This older man has approached him five times now, but so far Philip has been able to run into the night and escape.

This older man tries to coax Philip into coming with him across the highway into the dark area; if Philip follows, the man will give him some money. Philip knows in his heart that what this man wants is wrong, and he is very afraid. But where can Philip run for safety? He is alone in the thick of night, surrounded by a "huge pulsing animal that feeds on the weak, and swallows up the little ones of the street." Maybe next week Philip will be very hungry—hungry enough to take money from the man with the radio.[4]

The smaller boys receive serious beatings and get stabbed by robbers, who could be older street children. It is not uncommon for a smaller boy or girl to be asked to hand over their money to older boys. If the children refuse, they will be beaten and their money taken anyway. Street children do not get much protection from the police or the public. Often they do not report the beatings because they know the robbers will seek revenge.

The girls are more vulnerable. They are not only beaten but also raped. There is an existing mentality that girls who work or live on the street are readily available for sex. They are solicited for sex by delinquent boys and grown men. Refusal leads to beatings and rape. The men seek out the younger girls since it is a widely-held belief that there is a lesser chance of acquiring AIDS from younger children.

Another common form of abuse is the customer's refusal to pay for the children's work. It is discouraging for the children to work hard, long hours with the promise of compensation and then have their requests for payment refused. Even more frustrating is that there is little the children can do to prevent or fight this treatment.

Health problems

It is not difficult to observe the health problems children face when working on the streets. Overexposure to the cold or the sun causes headaches and nasal bleeding. Lack of sanitary facilities and poor personal hygiene result in bowel infections. Children often fall carrying heavy items or are struck by vehicles as they dodge in and out of heavy traffic selling their merchandise.

Usually the children do not receive medical treatment. They cannot afford to pay for such care. To receive free government medical services, the children have to bring a letter from the local administration. The children either do not have a home address or are afraid to apply.

Sex and survival

The lifestyle they are forced to live makes street children prime targets for sexual exploitation. Prostitution, seen as an opportunity for immediate income, has become a predominant means of survival. The prostitution of boys is now no more unusual than that of girls.

Those engaged in prostitution face many hazards that often result in death, not survival. Both boys and girls engaged in prostitution are constantly exposed to the lethal AIDS virus and other emotionally and physically crippling sexually transmitted diseases. Children lack vital information and education on sexual issues, such as birth control and conception. A survey indicated that many children thought that sleeping with more than one partner prevented them from becoming pregnant.

Once the girls become pregnant they often try traditional, unsafe methods of abortion, which often result in severe birth injuries, infections or other serious health problems. Since the streets are a hostile environment in which to raise a baby, it is common for those who do give birth to witness the death of their babies from cold and sickness. Either way, the children

35

usually experience deep emotional trauma, health problems and ensuing guilt.

Omer van Renterghem[5] states that, "Survival sex, international sex tourism and sexual abuse affect the lives of millions of children living in poverty worldwide." Children often become victims of adult sexual exploitation and are sexually active among themselves.

Gangs and survival

Despite the degradation, brutality and chaos, life on the street can seem appealing to many children in comparison to their home situations, where the threat of violence is just as constant as life on the streets. Sudip Mazumdar[6] describes a situation in Rio where a fifteen-year-old boy was beaten so badly at home that his sternum pierced his heart, killing him almost instantly.

Mazumdar reflected that "even when there is no physical abuse, the kids can go wanting for affection and attention. So they drift away to the streets, partly in search of the next best thing—tribal identity."

Membership in street gangs is a defense mechanism to ensure survival in a hostile environment. A gang provides the children with a degree of physical and emotional security. It also provides the protection, comradeship, status and sense of belonging of a substitute family. The rules to which the children subscribe are ones with which they can conform. Gang membership also meets the need for a sense of identity and self worth.

Violence and survival

Stealing, violence and fighting are considered the norm for survival on terror-filled streets. The children know the fear of brutality at the hands of others, fear of disease and disablement, fear of the police, fear of prison or being "put away." Violent behavior is often a logical consequence of the violence the children experienced in their families. Fierce competition on the streets, with activities jealously controlled and monitored by "territorial rights" of an unspoken hierarchy, also add to the landscape of violence that confronts the children daily.

With violence considered a significant tactic for day-to-day survival, the streets have truly become a combat zone where, in the children's intense struggle for life, only the fittest survive.

What other attitude can they have?

Having been let down at every turn and written off by society in general, many street children hold their community's standards, values and possessions in utter contempt. How can they respect a society that has deserted them—tossed them away as so much garbage? The community has left them to survive with little or no access to medical facilities, living in abject poverty, without labor laws to provide protection of their rights, in the worst kind of slum housing (if any), with a lack of educational opportunities and with other flagrant forms of neglect.

The children cannot afford, nor do they desire, to risk allowing such an uncaring society to dictate their means and methods of survival. From their point of view, whatever the job they perform or engage in on the streets, the name of the game is survival: from day to day and from hour to hour.

NOTES

1   Ethiopia's Ministry of Labor and Social Affairs and UNICEF; University College Cork, Ireland (1993): *Study on Street Children in Four Selected Towns of Ethiopia*. Addis Ababa, Ethiopia.

2   Ibid.

3   "Executive Director of UNICEF, James Grant, addresses 2nd International Conference on Street Youth in Rio de Janeiro: Call for Worldwide Alliances on Every Level to Strengthen Services for Youth," in *Esperanza* Vol. 5, Winter/Spring 1993, pp. 1-2.

4   Jon Detweiler, "Action on the Streets," in *Action Magazine* (Vol. 1, No. 1, 1992), pp. 1-3.

5   Omer van Renterghem, "Surviving the Streets," in *AIDS Action* (Issue 11, August 1990). Appropriate Health Resources and Technologies Action Group LTD. (AHRTAG).

5   Mazumdar Sudip, "My Streets: A World of Violence," in *Newsweek* (May 1, 1989), pp. 12-13.

PART TWO:

Street Life
and
Childhood
Development

4

Restoring fragile bonds: Bonding and attachment issues

Carole A. McKelvey

You have read the tragic anecdotes of street children in previous chapters. Sadly, these are just a few among a multitude of such children living on the world's danger-filled streets.
Daily thousands more children are left abandoned and helpless
by adults from whom they had expected love and protection.

When driven to live on the streets, the fragile bonds that
link the children to society become broken. Attachments with
their immediate families, their extended families and their
communities have been struck asunder.

Like children living in institutions, they look for comfort
and support from other children, from friends. They form what
are called "bond groups." But these groups do not suffice for
the attachments they need in their lives.

When the bonds and attachments children have with their
primary caregivers are broken, so are the children. They are the
faceless victims who may suffer the most trauma in a society of
hate and crime.

Even if they are not orphaned, many street children are
broken in spirit. These are horror stories. Horror stories about

children who have been lost, who are psychologically abused, neglected and mistreated to the degree that they no longer can love or trust any adult.

The most important thing that can happen to a child in the first critical years of life—other than having proper nutrition—is attachment to a primary caregiver. For many of the tiny victims of poverty and split families, this attachment has been broken. Generally the most psychological damage is done to children under the age of two, but older children also suffer the consequences of broken attachments.

In many cases of separated families, the lost children and grandchildren have no one they can count on for help. Children with attachment issues are rampant in the world of the streets. These unattached children, who may grow up without supportive homes and in a chaotic atmosphere of drugs and prostitution, can eventually become tomorrow's sociopaths.

This is especially true of children who grow up in the exploitative atmosphere of the streets where they are victimized by almost every adult they meet—the police, the pimps, other men or women who find profit from them; it is a hostile environment. These children grow up surrounded by turmoil, never knowing peace.

When trash and glue cans are children's playthings and they learn aggression and exploitation from their elders, how is a child to grow up right? When your model is a thug or a pimp, what possible outcome can there be?

When a young child becomes unattached, when that fragile bond is broken with their primary caregiver (usually the mother), children display distinct symptoms. These symptoms can render them unable to love, unable to live a normal life.

The loss of attachment can occur as they are sent from the arms of those whom they once trusted to take care of them. In the place of trust come fear and anger. When this happens in a chaotic situation, it usually means these victims are constantly on the move—from one place to another—constantly experiencing "bonding breaks." Many of these children can become what is clinically known as "character-disordered."

Those caring for them need to know what to look for and

what they need to do for a child who may have an attachment disorder.

Symptoms of character-disturbed children

Specific symptoms[1] to look for, even in very young children, include:

- Lack of ability to give and receive affection
- Self-destructive behavior
- Cruelty to others or to pets
- Phoniness
- Stealing, hoarding and gorging
- Speech pathology
- Extreme control problems
- Lack of long-term childhood friends
- Seeing their caregivers as unreasonable and angry
- Abnormalities in eye contact
- Preoccupation with blood, fire and gore
- Superficial attractiveness and friendliness with strangers
- Learning disorders
- Crazy lying

With the diagnosis of attachment disorders comes a new set of behavioral problems. Says specialist Selma Frailberg:[2]

> When, for any reason, a child has spent the whole or a large part of his or her infancy in an environment that could not provide him or her with human partners or the conditions for sustained human attachments, the later development of the child demonstrates measurable effects. For example:
>
> - The children form relationships only on the basis of need, with little regard for one caregiver over another;
>
> - There is an impairment of the capacity to attach to any person;
>
> - There is also retardation, which continues in follow-up testing. Conceptual thinking remains low, even when favorable environments are provided for the children in the second and third years of life. Language itself, which was grossly retarded in all the infant studies, improves under more favorable environmental conditions, but this area of learning is never fully regained; and

♦ Disorders of impulse control, particularly in the area of aggression, were reported in all follow-up studies of these children.

Experts know that an attachment problem can manifest itself in children who are orphaned or otherwise estranged from their caregivers as small infants. Potential bonding problems in small infants, however, are easier to address than in older children who have suffered bonding breaks before the age of two. With proper intervention, including "holding" techniques or "holding" therapy,[3] new caregivers can lead a baby to an emotional attachment to them.

With older children, however, the loss of trust at an early age is very difficult to overcome. Sometimes extensive therapy—often unavailable and unattainable because of costs—is the only answer to forming a bond with such a child.

The key, experts say, is having one consistent nurturing caregiver available to the child during the formative first two years, even if those years occur in the midst of poverty or a split-apart family.

A lack of attachment affects children's ability to form close relationships throughout their lives. It is an affectionate bond between two individuals which endures through time and space and serves to join them emotionally.

Attachment, literally, helps a child to:[4]

♦ Attain full intellectual potential;
♦ Sort out what is perceived;
♦ Think logically;
♦ Develop a conscience;
♦ Become self-reliant;
♦ Cope with stress and frustration;
♦ Handle fear and worry;
♦ Develop future relationships; and
♦ Reduce jealousy.

We can help many of these children who have attachment disorders with adequate therapy, but the number of children currently receiving adequate treatment is minuscule. Early intervention and treatment are rare and too many substitute caregivers do not understand attachment disorders or recognize the symptoms.[5]

Many mental health problems of street children come from their removal from their family of origin and their subsequent movement through the social services system. This is why those working with children of the streets must be prepared to offer these children stability. The best cure for attachment disorders, other than adequate therapy, is a consistent, nurturing caregiver who is committed to the child for the long term.

Multiple moves, or "breaks," cause the greatest wounds to a child's psyche. These breaks can cause the condition we have been talking about—"attachment disorders."

Attachment disorders

Among the most difficult children to rear are older children who have suffered from attachment disorders because of their early childhood experiences. These children have not made that critical connection with a primary caregiver that is so important during their first years of life. The result can be severe. This is true even if the child has been removed from the chaotic atmosphere of street life and found the stability of an institution for his or her care.

The people of Covenant House (the largest international agency serving homeless and runaway youth) in New York City are like many others around the world who work to rescue street children who have had their childhood cruelly snatched from them. They hope to take these unattached children and bring them into a world of caring, where they can learn again to trust and love. For many young people on the streets, the only solution is to make stable, healthy, lasting connections to other caring persons. Some will need therapy to overcome their abuse and neglect.

One of the therapies that has proven helpful for such children is known as "holding therapy." This therapy consists of a series of controlled "holdings" that brings out control issues and confronts them.

Because this therapy is confrontational, it remains controversial in some areas of the psychiatric community, but has proven very effective for children with severe attachment dis-

45

orders. Many children who have been subjected to sexual abuse, no matter how young, can eventually become perpetrators of sexual abuse or prostitutes. Their anger and rage take them down the same road that hurt them so deeply. It is the only way they know how to hurt those around them, and for some it is the only way they know to make a living.

During the holdings unattached children, who cannot stand closeness and touch, become extremely agitated when their control of a situation is threatened. During this agitation, a therapist can gently guide these children to confront the rage that boils just under the surface. Why rage? The child is full of rage due to unresolved needs as a young child, when he or she felt hopeless and helpless and hurt.

Once the therapist has guided the child through this "rage reaction," the child is vulnerable and open to rebonding. During this opportunity the therapist sensitively leads the child to a bond with the therapist, in a loving way.

Later, after more work on control issues and getting the rage worked out of the child, the therapist can bond the child to a trained therapeutic foster parent. Once a child has bonded to someone, it is a matter of transferring that bond to the appropriate caregiver.

The attachment cycle

Psychologists and psychiatrists are just beginning to realize the crisis created by a lack of attachment. Many children of the streets have suffered from abuse—that abuse may be sexual or it may take the form of physical or mental abuse. All these can cause bonding breaks and render a child unattached.

When considering a substitute caregiver for a child who has suffered bonding and attachment breaks, it is important to note that the primary caregiver can take several forms—it can be the birth mother or father, foster mother or father, an adoptive parent, or someone else who can provide consistency in the child's life. The key is to have one consistent caregiver who can be a source of permanence for the child, who can give that child an anchor in the stormy sea of life.

In a normal childhood in a loving, consistent family, a child gets this anchor during the first two years. It is through the attachment cycle that an infant first attaches to a primary caregiver and, subsequently, to society. This two-year-cycle[6] is the key to healthy attachments later in life (see Figure 4.1 below).

During the attachment cycle an infant experiences a *need*—either pain, hunger or discomfort—and expresses that need through a rage reaction that elicits a response from the primary caregiver to *gratify* that need. It is important that the caregiver gratify this need with touch, eye contact, motion or food.

The repetition of this cycle of gratification, thousands of times during the first two years, without interruption, results in the formation of a strong trust bond between the child and caregiver. The bond of trust and attachment later enables the child to accept the limits and controls the parents impose.

This bond of trust is a fragile one; it is easily broken and an interruption of the cycle can occur when there is:

◆ Separation from, or change of, the primary caregiver.

◆ Abuse or neglect.

◆ Chronic and unrelieved pain.

◆ Gratification without touch, motion or eye-contact.

Any one of these interruptions can cause a bonding break in a child living in a poverty-stricken or disruptive situation.

Figure 4.1. The attachment cycle

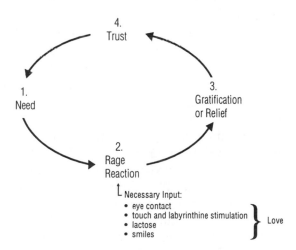

Children who have experienced interruptions of the attachment cycle during the first two years of life may exhibit some symptoms of attachment-disordered children later in life as described above.

A major problem with children is correctly identifying their attachment issues. Foster Cline, a psychiatrist and teacher, says: "What many people do not understand is that a very disturbed child is unlikable. The disturbance makes it hard to like the kid, even though you love him and want to love him to pieces. And these [unattached] kids know how to play the victim role," he says. "It's always, 'poor me.' So what happens is they really may be victims, but that is no excuse for their behavior."[7]

Psychologist Barbara Rila, a founder of the national group ATTACh (Association for Treatment and Training in the Attachment of Children), emphasizes that it is important to know the history of a child.[8] With access to the child's history, those working with the child may learn why this child has ongoing psychological disabilities, such as those described above.

In a confused street situation, gaining access to the child's history will be difficult, but it is worth the effort. The history can also offer the therapist clues on how to begin the rebonding process.

An unattached first year of life gets children off to a very bad start. If you add the trauma of abandonment and broken hearts to that, the result can be very disturbed children with many problems.

A newly released study shows the extent of the damage as found in a group of adopted children who had suffered bonding breaks at an early age. The study looked at deviant behaviors, including the symptoms of attachment-disturbed children described earlier in this chapter.

Researchers wanted to find out at what age problem behaviors first appeared. They found the problematical behaviors did not show up significantly until the children reached adolescence. They believed that deviant behaviors were connected in some way to the adoptions of the studied children and the bonding breaks they suffered.

Although not a clinical study, J. Lynn Rhodes and Ellis P. Copeland found the "roots of the behavior may lie in early life experiences, but the fruit is not produced until adolescence." The information on the high percentage of deviancy was found to be "revealing to the point of being shocking."

Although no such study has been done to date on children abandoned on the streets, I believe this information comparing birth children and adopted children who suffer from bonding breaks is relevant in any such discussion (see Table 4.1 below).

Many of the children studied showed significant evidence of attachment disorders that stem from multiple bonding breaks in infancy (probably caused by moves in foster care). It is still not known how many breaks it takes before a child is sure to have attachment difficulties. In a situation in which a child is on the streets—either because the child was "thrown away" or chose to leave because of abuse or neglect—the author speculates it may not take many breaks, because of the trauma caused by the situation itself.

We cannot cure the problems of children with attachment disorders by gentle holdings, hugs and kisses. These children need more than love, especially those who have experienced the worst the streets have to offer.

Many unattached children need intensive long-term therapy, such as the holding techniques described earlier in this chapter, related to the rebonding process. In therapy it is important to bring out the behaviors that resulted in the attachment disorders. Then the therapist can deal with specific causes and help the child to begin to heal.

Table 4.1. Survey of dysfunctional behavior in children[9]

BEHAVIORS	BIRTH (%)	ADOPTED (%)
Inability to give or receive affection	3.2	21.3
Phoniness	1.9	15.1
Self-control problems	3.9	26.3
Lack of long-term friends	4.5	21.9
Lying	3.9	25.7
Rejection of authority	1.3	30.0
Refusal to follow parental guidelines	3.2	25.8
Manipulation of others	2.6	23.8

"Traumatic incidents have a direct and concrete result in subsequent traumas and the child's emotional behavior," says Barbara Rila. . . . "A second major reason to know the past is that children base later relationships on the earlier model of the original family."[10] If sexual abuse is suspected in a child, it is even more important that the child's caregivers know this information. Children with attachment disorders based on sexual abuse often become perpetrators themselves, as a result of the abuse.

"With the help of a qualified therapist, the caregivers can help a child cope with the aftermath of abuse. What works with one child may not work with others. We need to empower parents and professionals to parent children with attachment issues," says Rila.[11]

Connell Watkins, a child therapist and specialist in attachment issues, claims continuity is the key to helping children so traumatized: "Continuity and a stable place to call their own, a place they can go back to and get special treatment is so important. But the basic need is the continuity."[12]

Author's suggestions

It is particularly important that those deciding on the fate of such a child consider specific guidelines regarding child development and rule accordingly. These guidelines include:[13]

◆ The emotional state of the child;
◆ The nature of the attachment between the substitute caregivers and the child;
◆ The nature of the attachment with the birth parents; and
◆ The environment that will best match the needs of the child.

The goal should be to provide stable, caring, supportive parents for these needy children.

Only with the early intervention of a committed, nurturing caregiver can a child avoid the horror of attachment disorders. Those who work with children from the streets need to allow for this. Good parenting and a positive environment seem to help children overcome bad beginnings and become all they can be, despite the influence of the streets and other abuses.

A healthy sign, and one to be encouraged, is when older children can transfer their bond to another caregiver when separated from their families. For when a child has bonded with one caregiver it is possible to transfer that bond, even in the midst of the uncertainties of street life, to another.

The author urges parents and professionals alike who are working with an emotionally challenged child to get to know as much as possible about the child's background and any genetic factors that may be influencing the child's behavior. With proper professional guidance it is possible to rescue a badly challenged child.

These children, however, must be placed in a predictable, positive environment. At the heart of the solution is the careful matching of these children to reliable attachment figures who can be committed for the long term to healing them.

Cautions

The following are some pitfalls for caregivers to avoid when dealing with children of the streets.

Children placed randomly and repeatedly. A system that shuffles children and babies from place to place with little regard for the outcome must be corrected.

The system must keep track of children and plan permanent homes from the minute it is determined they are abandoned. Parents—adoptive and foster—must be given the tools they need, during matching and pre- and post-placement counseling, to stay with a challenged child. These are very difficult children to raise and parent.

It will be up to substitute caregivers, and social and adoption workers, to keep track of the children and hasten this permanency planning. These people must also be the advocates for their small charges.

Inadequate knowledge among professionals. In another arena, often the therapeutic community is undereducated when it comes to bonding and attachment issues; many do not recognize or properly diagnose damaged children. Additional educational efforts are needed to give therapists working with unattached children the tools they need to provide help.

What happens over time when these unattached children finally find a secure place? What solutions are there for those substitute caregivers who discover, over time, that the children they have brought into their homes suffer from the effects of attachment disorder?

These parents with very difficult children may have to use strict parenting methods. They may have to handle the children in a firm manner (such as "tough love") to make them responsible in the future.

Street children have taken a journey along a path that has shocked and shaken their very foundations. During this journey, with its multiple bonding breaks and moves, many of these already hurting children have also developed emotional disabilities and mental challenges. Making the situation even worse is the inability of substitute caregivers to respond. Clearly, every child needs a permanent and safe home:

◆ A home where they can be matched to parents[14] and feel nurtured, safe and loved; and

◆ A home where they can heal and grow.

Those planning to rear or give substitute care to these children with special needs must have the knowledge and long-term support to provide a nurturing environment.

As an aftermath of their experiences on the street, many children have come to mistrust others. The older children are the ones agencies have had trouble fitting into a family. These children (ages 9 to 19) must be placed in a predictable, positive environment with a reliable attachment figure.

The type of care these "special needs" children require includes:

◆ Loving, responsive parents who can provide consistent discipline and who can deal with the child's fear, uncertainty and rejecting behavior;

◆ Parents with enough pre- and post-placement counseling that they are prepared for the problems that will arise;

◆ Parents who have been matched in temperament to their new charges; and

◆ Parents who can understand and relate to the sort of problem this child will likely bring with him or her.

In the past, many workers have failed to give the full picture of the problems to substitute parents. When this deception happens, parents are unlikely to acknowledge the grieving process. For future caregivers to be able to help street children with these special needs, they will need to know what the children they are caring for have suffered.

NOTES

1   Foster Cline, *What Shall We Do with this Child?* (Evergreen, Colorado: Youth Behavior Program, 1979).

2   S. Frailberg, *Every Child's Birthright: In Defense of Mothering* (New York: Basic Books, 1977), pp. 51-54.

3   Many babies and young children benefit from a technique called "holding," in which the caregiver holds the child in a gentle, nurturing way so that the child is able to receive the caregiver's love while maintaining eye contact. This technique is taught in *Holding Time* by Martha Welch (Simon & Schuster, 1988).

4   Frailberg, p. 28.

5   Magid and McKelvey, *High Risk: Children without a Conscience* (New York: Bantam Books, 1988).

6   Carole A. McKelvey and JoEllen Stevens, *Adoption Crisis* (Golden, Colorado: Fulcrum Press, 1994).

7   Foster Cline, personal interview, January 1991.

8   Barbara Rila, personal interview, Atlanta, Georgia, U.S.A., July 1991.

9   J. Lynn Rhodes and Ellis P. Copeland, "Dysfunctional Behavior in Adopted Children: Behavior Differences between Adopted and Birth Children" (University of Northern Colorado, November 1991). Reprinted with permission. A survey conducted with a Christian adoption group that had placed more than 900 children in the past twenty years. The 388 adopted children and 290 birth children tested lived throughout the U.S.A.

10   Rila, personal interview, July 1991.

11   Ibid. Rila says that is the basis for the group ATTACh (Asso-

ciation for Treatment and Training in the Attachment of Children). For more information on ATTACh, you may contact the group by writing ATTACh, 2775 VillaCreek, #240, Dallas, Texas, 75234 U.S.A.

12 Connell Watkins and Associates, Evergreen, Colorado, U.S.A., provides therapy, consultation and training regarding attaching issues.

13 Magid and McKelvey, 1988, p. 334.

14 For information on matching and the SAME (Stevens Adopt Match Evaluator) matching instrument, write to Dr. JoEllen Stevens, P.O. Box 1133, Oakview, California, 93022 U.S.A.

5

Healing deep emotional wounds

Thea W. Wilshire

If a child has a broken arm or a crushed foot, the area of injury is identified easily and the course of intervention is widely known. But how would one detect and treat a broken heart? What does crushed self-esteem look like and can it be remedied? Though emotional wounds might appear invisible at first glance, children do exhibit signs and symptoms of emotional trauma. With training and increased awareness, street workers can begin to recognize these indicators of emotional woundedness and intervene.

This chapter begins by focusing on the various reasons psychological wounds must be addressed in working with street children. Next, the types of emotional issues that street life raises for children and adolescents will be examined, with particular attention given to the sources of trauma and forms of emotional woundedness that may be seen. The chapter closes with words of encouragement and direction for those who are working with or want to minister to the emotional needs of street children.

Why bother?

Emotional needs may be harder to detect than the more

55

basic survival needs of shelter, food and clothing. Further, with limited resources and overwhelming needs, psychological interventions for "invisible" needs may take lowest priority in the street worker's mind. It is essential, however, to consider psychological issues in the care of street children and adolescents because they have a serious impact on more than just the emotional health of the children; they also affect the children's physical health, self-esteem, social connections and spiritual growth. To further explain how psychological issues affect more than emotional health, a brief focus will be given to each of these less obvious areas.

Physical

There are many ways to study the body. One of the newer scientific ways of understanding how the body functions examines how the central nervous system, the immune system and hormones work together to regulate the body. In greatly simplified terms, this field (psychoneuroimmunology) examines the connection between our emotional and physical states. It looks at how emotional factors, such as depression or anxiety, can have an impact on a person's physical health and immune functioning. Research suggests that our physical and emotional health are much more closely linked than was previously imagined.

For street children, this translates to poorer physical health when psychological needs and incidents of emotional trauma are not addressed. It also means that work on increasing psychological well-being will more than likely correlate with increased physical well-being and health. If for no other reason than this, outreach to street children must include emotional as well as physical interventions.

Quality of life and social networks

Even as psychological factors affect physical health, they also influence the quality of life experienced by an individual. Such diverse factors as self-esteem, confidence and achievement determine a person's quality of life. An abandoned street child, a depressed street adolescent or children ravaged by sexual abuse or fears for their physical safety will likely lack self-esteem and confidence, have insufficient achievement in school (if they attend) and will be experiencing less than the abundant life God desires for them.

56

Similarly, just as psychological factors influence a person's quality of life, social networks also have an impact on self-esteem, confidence, achievement and morality. Social connectedness is a critical dynamic in forming a personal identity, for it is through the reactions and feelings of significant others that an individual begins to develop a self-concept. Street children lack mature and reliable social connections and usually have poor resolution of self-identity issues and tragically low self-concepts.

The disciplines of sociology, anthropology and psychology all emphasize the importance of social communities and state that we are who we are because of our connections with others in a variety of arenas (such as family, peers, friends, coworkers and society). Street children usually lack connections to the more traditional experiences of community; if they do not, they experience these networks in a very negative manner—as marginalized and unwanted members of society.

While most street children lack the traditional social networks of family, school and church, they meet their needs of acceptance and belonging by creating their own social commu nities on the streets. Many of these "societies within society" are complete with their own rules and values. These communities, however, are marked by disorganization and inconsistency. It is doubtful that these street communities serve as good contexts for teaching and modeling higher levels of moral development and personal growth.

Spiritual

Finally, in addition to physical health and quality of life factors, psychological factors also influence an individual's spiritual life. A person's emotional development and their past trauma history are intimately connected to their ability to experience God's love. Ana-Marie Rizutto[1] has done groundbreaking work on how children form their understanding of God or their "God concept." She found that the internalized early experiences that individuals have with parents or authority figures provide the basis for how a person will experience God and develop spiritually.

For street children this means that if they have experienced parental abandonment, abuse or neglect then they will probably consciously or unconsciously expect God the Father to treat them in a similar manner. If they have experienced very judgmental or vindictive caregivers, they likely will anticipate God's character to be this way, too. Through prayer, compassion and psychological interventions that address their early experiences as well as their current conceptions of God, street children can be given the freedom to know God in spirit and truth.

The emotional health of a child has an impact on more than just the psychological arena of life—it touches upon the child's physical and spiritual well-being as well as influences the child's quality of life. Consequently, we must add intervention for the emotional traumas and needs of street children to our ministry strategies. God knows the connections between emotional, physical and spiritual development. He can work miracles of instant psychological healing or he may orchestrate slower processes of emotional healing. As a minister to street children, God can use you to bring about emotional, physical and spiritual healing.

What does a broken heart look like?

If we agree that psychological issues are worth considering and can have an impact on our interventions in the lives of children living on the street, what's next? Psychology is a big field and can seem overwhelming if taken as a whole. What may make it more manageable is to narrow the focus in working with street children to two areas: specific sources of psychological trauma for street children and types of symptoms or forms of emotional illness that street children may exhibit. When a street worker can use information from these two areas, they can highlight and give special attention to the children who have the greatest need for psychological intervention.

Sources of trauma

There are many sources or causes of emotional trauma for street children. Unfortunately, for many children, this includes both on-street and pre-street events. The following list gives some issues that professionals working with street children have found have the most impact on a child's emotional well-being:

- abandonment or being forced out of the home
- being disrespected or physically attacked by authority figures (parents, police, military, business people)
- death of a loved one
- domestic violence
- drug use (usually involving 2-3 drugs simultaneously)
- emotional deprivation and a lack of nurturance
- extremely disruptive household
- parental substance abuse or other forms of mental illness in their parents (depression, thought disorders)
- physical and sexual abuse
- poor nutrition and compromised health
- poverty and economic destitution
- removal of birth children from street adolescents
- sexually transmitted disease, prostitution, rape
- stress of street survival
- systemic abuse and neglect (in child welfare system)
- witnessing violence (including the murder of friends, relatives or parents)

Besides the sources of emotional stress and trauma listed above, some people have underlying, genetic predispositions toward acquiring certain forms of mental illness (such as depression, thought disorders, problems with extreme mood swings and anxiety disorders). This means that some emotional problems "run in families" and can be passed on to children— even when they are not living with their parents. While it is hard to predict which individuals in a family will be emotionally ill, researchers have found that certain factors make at-risk children more vulnerable or likely to become mentally ill. Extreme stress, like that found while living on the street, may push children over the edge into the abyss of mental illness.

Further, children are strongly affected when one or both of their parents are emotionally disturbed. In the past, street children were viewed as *runaways* who were out of their homes because of their own individual choices. Currently, with the understanding that some parents abandon or force children out of the home, different distinctions are being made between children who are *runaways* and those who are *throwaways*. With this in mind, familial dysfunction, rather than individual dysfunction, can be seen as the precursor to street life. Thus, for many street children, we can understand the process of their leaving home as an adaptive response to abuse, poverty, violence, drugs and parental emotional problems.

F. Peralta[2] makes the observation that street children of Western or industrialized countries are often pushed out of their homes because of neglect and abuse, while many Latin American street children are on the streets primarily as workers in an informal economy.

While this section outlines many types of stress and trauma that street children may experience, it seems important to note this listing is not meant to be a description of the experiences of all street children. Further, the same disclaimer applies when you read the next section describing the symptoms or types of emotional illness commonly found among street children.

All of the following variations of emotional problems will not be present in all street children. Each child's background, experience on the streets and response to street stressors will be unique and the overall population of street children constitute a much more diverse group than many may think. Some researchers say it is arrogant to propose a "street child profile," and warn that prevailing stereotypes and negative labeling can be used politically to justify violence against street children.[3]

Types of symptoms and forms of emotional illness

If you were organizing a medical station in an isolated area, would you prefer to know that the people in the area were "sick" or that they were suffering specifically from poisonous snake bites, anemia, leprosy and cholera? The more specific the information you receive, particularly if it included diagnoses and incidence rates, the better you can plan your interventions and organize your limited resources. The same applies to psychological needs and interventions.

Most of the current international reports coming from workers interacting with street children are at the same level as a medical report saying people are "sick." The few workers who include emotional factors in their writing describe the children as "depressed" or "delayed." These descriptors are fairly generic, however, and are usually not based on findings from objective tests and measures or on the strict definitions of professional diagnostic criterion.

To date, most of the limited empirical studies of emotional and behavioral problems among street children have been conducted in the U.S.A. and Canada. Further, most of these studies have focused on runaway and homeless children and adolescents (usually in shelters). The reports in the literature on street children in South America, Central America, Africa and Southeast Asia are usually descriptive or subjective reports.

In an attempt to focus on more objective information, most of the data in this next section comes from studies that focused on Western or Anglo-American homeless and street children, unless otherwise noted. In an interesting comparison between South African street children and American runaways, however, L. Richter[4] concludes that these two groups share many similarities (their backgrounds, their experiences on the streets and their future potential). So the following statistics of emotional difficulties in street children could be applicable across cultures and continents.

Reports on the types or forms of emotional problems among street children have included anxiety, attention and concentration difficulties, cognitive delay, conduct disorders, depression, destructiveness, developmental delay, learning disabilities, oppositionality and aggression, post-traumatic stress disorder (PTSD), school problems, sexual acting out, sexual identity problems, somatic complaints, substance abuse problems and suicide attempts. To illustrate how widespread these problems are among street children, specific incident rates from various studies are listed below.

In a study of emotional and behavioral disorders of homeless and runaway youth in New York City conducted by Covenant House,[5] it was discovered that out of 150 street children interviewed 41% reported abusing alcohol and/or drugs, 59% met the criterion for a diagnosis of conduct disorder, 49% had a major mood disorder, 52% reported a manic episode (a period of very high energy and feelings of euphoric well-being), 37% reported chronic clinical depression and 32% met the criterion for post-traumatic stress disorder. Forty-one percent said they had considered suicide and 27% had attempted it, some more than once. Further, street youth that were beaten, sexually molested or had a child were more likely to attempt suicide.

Among street children in Johannesburg, nearly 40% showed evidence of the clinical symptomatology of depression.[6] In a study of homeless children (4-10 years old) in New York City, 80% demonstrated visual-motor integration problems and 79% displayed serious cognitive delay.[7] Slower development and cognitive delay were noted in homeless school-age children (6-12 years old) and preschoolers (3-5 years old) in Philadelphia. The preschoolers also demonstrated significantly elevated scores on measures of aggression, conduct problems, destructiveness, anxiety, depression and somatic complaints.[8]

What now?

After reading the material in this chapter, the author hopes you will have a greater awareness of the emotional effects of street life on children. Just being aware of the psychological welfare of children, however, does not address the needs directly. So what do you do with this new understanding? Unfortunately, this brief chapter cannot provide street workers with all of the information needed to psychologically treat children—that would require a full library and concentrated training. Yet, this does not mean the worker is powerless to begin addressing the emotional needs of street children.

You can begin to address psychological issues by asking children about their pre-street life as well as on-street experiences. You can recognize and validate the impact of street life and help the children see it, too. You can use your knowledge of psychological concerns to bring other perspectives into planning and conceptualization meetings for street children ministries. You can search out and petition for team members (or professionals, if they are available in your region or community) with psychological training. You can familiarize yourself with psychological intervention programs currently in place in other ministries. Most important, you can pray for the emotional needs and growth of the children with whom you work.

If you are interested, you can read material, attend seminars and register for classes that will provide more training in the various forms of psychological therapy available for use with children. Because children do not focus on verbal communication to the extent that adults do, you may find more effective means of intervention in individual play therapy, sibling or cohort play therapy, art therapies or therapeutic storytelling activities.

Awareness of the psychological needs of street children is a great starting point for understanding and working with each individual teenager or child you serve. For example, if a person is physically ill or injured, you would be less likely to take their negative comments as personal attacks, but could see such behavior as the result of the person's physical condition at that time. Similarly, you might take less personally the irritability an adolescent displays toward you on the street or in the shelter and understand their conduct more as an outcropping of their underlying emotional pain.

In another example, understanding that children may use sexual contact as a way to provide intimacy or as an attempt to make sense of sexual abuse they have suffered, you would be less likely to address sexual practices as moral or spiritual issues. Although you need to address sexual problems, you can now do so with an understanding of why the child or teen may be sexually involved and so you can deal more compassionately and more appropriately with meeting the individual's need for intimacy.

The best way to intervene and provide for the psychological needs of street children is to prevent them from arriving on the streets in the first place. This can be done in a variety of ways: politically, with government benefits and subsidies; economically, with jobs and housing; and working with the families and through various community interventions. Because family concerns are perhaps most directly connected with children arriving on the streets, programs targeting abuse prevention and teaching positive parenting skills are sorely needed.

By providing services to street children, we give them opportunities to move out of their current situations and ask them to consider running the race of life with those of us who are gifted with greater financial, physical, emotional and spiritual resources. Do not, however, expect someone to run a marathon with a fractured leg or foot. Similarly, we must not overlook the invisible fractures and wounds of emotional trauma when providing services to street children.

Concluding comments

Life on the streets has many negative effects on children and adolescents. Street life affects children's physical health through exposure to violence, illness, drug use and sexually-transmitted diseases. The poor nutrition and lack of educational opportunities associated with street life delays or permanently damages a child's physical and cognitive development.

Without caring authority figures to model morality, children develop in a vacuum and have difficulty showing moral behavior. Street life can have very injurious emotional effects on children. And the stress and traumas associated with pre-street and on-street experiences can stunt spiritual growth.

NOTES

1   Ana-Marie Rizutto, *The Birth of the Living God: A Psychoanalytic Study* (Chicago: The University of Chicago Press, 1979).

2   F. Peralta, "Children of the Streets of Mexico," in *Children and Youth Services Review* (14), pp. 347-362.

3   W. De Oliveira, M. Baizerman and L. Pellet, "Street Children in Brazil and their Helpers: Comparative Views on Aspirations and the Future," in *International Social Work* (35), pp.163-176.

4   L. Richter, "South Africa 'Street Children': Comparisons with Anglo-American Runaways," in *Contemporary Issues in Cross-Cultural Psychology*. N. Bleichrodt and P.J.D. Drenth, eds. (Amsterdam, Netherlands: Swets & Zeitlinger, 1991), pp. 96-109.

5   B. Feitel, N. Margetson, J. Chamas and C. Lipman, "Psychosocial Background and Behavioral and Emotional Disorders of Homeless and Runaway Youth," in *Hospital and Community Psychiatry* (1992, No. 43), pp. 155-159.

6   L. Richter, 1991.

7   S. Fox, R. Barnett, M. Davies and H. Bird, "Psychopathology
     and Developmental Delay in Homeless Children: A Pilot
     Study," in *Journal of the American Academy of Child and Adoles-
     cent Psychiatry* (29), pp. 732-735.

8   L. Rescorla, R. Parker and P. Stolleym, "Ability, Achieve-
     ment, and Adjustment in Homeless Children," in *American
     Journal of Orthopsychiatry* (1991, No. 61), pp. 210-220.

6

Promoting moral growth
and development

Perry Downs

Children must learn right from wrong, and be willing to do right. Indeed, the health of a society rests to a large degree on its capacity to live according to principles of right and wrong. When the moral base of a society is lost, the society is doomed to failure.

Children living on city streets apart from parental or adult supervision, and fending for themselves by all available means, find it difficult to determine right from wrong. Treating children in unjust ways eliminates their capacity to understand the difference between right and wrong. How do we know right from wrong, and how can we help children learn right from wrong? What can we do to help children recover the ability to sort out right from wrong and make moral decisions based on what is right?

Basic definitions

Before we consider how to help children, we must be clear on definitions. Clarifying what we mean will help us do a better job of working with children in the area of their moral behavior.

Moral judgment and moral behavior

Moral judgment is how a child *thinks* about a moral issue. It is concerned with how a child decides what is right or wrong. Moral behavior is how a child *acts* concerning a moral issue, despite how he or she thinks about it. A common problem is that children's (and adults') moral behavior is not always consistent with their moral judgment. We are all prone to do things that we think are wrong, or fail to do things we think are right. Therefore, how we think and how we may act are two separate issues.

Moral choices and moral decisions

Moral choices are concerned with *what* a person believes to be right or wrong. Sometimes called "moral content," moral choices deal with the content or substance of a moral belief. When street children reason "stealing is not wrong," it is a statement of moral content because it states what they believe to be right or wrong.

Moral decisions are the basis of moral choices and are concerned with *why* a person believes a specific content. Sometimes called "moral structure," the decisions are rooted in a specific kind of moral reasoning. "Stealing is not wrong *because it is how I get my food*" is a moral content supported by a reason or structure. In working with street children we must understand the reasoning behind their moral choices, because it is in the reasoning that the potential for growth resides. Therefore, helping children develop morally is concerned with both *what* is right or wrong, and *why* it is right or wrong.

Morals and ethics

Morals are rules of behavior that are related to any society. They change from society to society, or can change over time within a society. Things that may be considered immoral in one society may not be immoral in another. For example, certain clothing styles may be acceptable in one culture, but be offensive in another. For a woman to bare her arms in most Western societies is not immoral, but would be considered immoral in many Muslim contexts. Morals are rooted in society and therefore change as society changes.

Ethics are principles of right and wrong that are always the same in every context and are not negotiable. They are "above" cultures and society and are always binding in all contexts. People may disagree on what these ethical guidelines are, but that they should exist is generally seen to be true.

The immense difficulty in working with children who have been living on the streets without adult nurture and discipline is that they have virtually lost their capacity to see and respond to either moral or ethical guidelines. Because these moral and ethical restraints have been violated in the lives of these children, they have difficulty understanding that they even exist. Even the broader, more foundational ethical guidelines of human living are lost so that the child cannot make even the most basic of moral choices. Basic behavioral limits such as lying, stealing, or even killing can become acceptable behaviors to persons who operate without moral or ethical principles. We must teach these children to think and behave according to moral guidelines.

The connections between knowing and doing

Helping persons grow morally is more than a matter of teaching them right from wrong. The simple teaching of moral content—what is right and wrong—will not necessarily change behavior. As we all know from our own life experience, knowing and doing are two different things. How does a person move from right thinking to right action?

First, a child must know right from wrong. We cannot expect children to do what they do not know. There is a place to teach children moral content so that they might know right from wrong.

For children who have been in a context without any moral teaching, this is a critical step. We must teach children that right and wrong exist, and "we" (the group with whom they are related) have standards and beliefs about what is right and wrong. We must communicate the truth of right and wrong.

Teaching moral content is best done in relationship. If there is an emotional bond forming between the child and an adult or group, the child will more easily accept the moral standards being taught. If children are loved, and can receive that love, they will be more likely to learn the values of the persons who love them. Children must feel related to a society in order to accept the morals of the society.

When children form gangs, the power of the gang to influence the child is rooted in the relationship which is established. Because the child now belongs to the group, the child will accept the patterns of right and wrong as determined by the gang. Whatever the gang advocates as "right" becomes "right" for that child.

But knowing right from wrong is not the same as doing the right thing. It is perfectly possible to know the right thing, but not be willing to do it. We can all remember times in our lives when we knew what we should do, but we simply did not want to do it. It was not a matter of moral knowledge, but a matter of moral will. Children must not only know what is right—they must also be willing to do what is right.

It is not true that all people are "good" and always want to do right. The brutality around us shows the great evil of which we are all capable. The corruption of our moral will is more than a matter of what the people around us have done to us; it is also a matter of human personality. We do not always want to do what is right. All human hearts have a rebellious spirit that may choose to do evil. The moral problems of street children run deeper than their environmental situation; like all of humankind, they are flawed at the deepest level of their human personality.

Helping children grow morally concerns the desires of their hearts as well as the information in their minds. Moral training that helps children must deal with their desire to do right along with the knowledge of what is right.

But it is possible for a child to know the right thing, want to do the right thing, and still not have the strength to do the right thing. They may lack the emotional or inner power to act on what they know and feel is right.

The apostle Paul described this condition in his own life when he wrote, "For I do not do what I want, but I do the very thing I hate" (Romans 7:15b). It is frustrating not to have the moral strength to act upon our own moral convictions.

The strength to act on convictions independently will be very weak in abused and victimized people. Strength to act on what they know is right comes more easily in a group than in individuals. If an entire group can be moved to behave in increasingly moral ways, the individuals will also be strengthened.

Stages of moral reasoning

The research in moral development suggests that there are three primary levels of moral reasoning through which each person will normally progress as he or she moves toward moral maturity. If a person is in a context that does not hinder moral development, the *structure* of moral reasoning will develop through three predictable stages. Although children living on the streets have probably been in a context that does not allow them to develop normally in their moral reasoning, it is helpful to understand what a normal pattern of development looks like. That will help us understand which level of moral reasoning we want to see the children get to as they begin to heal from the damaging consequences of street life.

Before they reach the first level of moral reasoning, very young children are pre-moral or simply not concerned with moral issues. Babies are not aware of any moral issues when they cry to be fed. Their only concern is their hunger. They do not consider any moral dimensions to their actions, and this is how it should be. They should be free to be babies, not yet concerned with issues of right and wrong.

As children move into early childhood, however, we expect them to have a sense of right and wrong. We expect behaviors from them that are in keeping with basic expectations of our society. We expect them to obey, to tell the truth and to be kind to those around them. If a child or an adult remains in the pre-moral state of infancy, we need to be concerned. Such children and adults are threats to society because they have no internal limitations on their behavior. Such a person can injure or kill and never feel remorse. It is not good to remain at the pre-moral state.

Level one judgments

The first level of moral reasoning, called *pre-conventional*, focuses only on self and personal concerns. "Good" is that which serves me well, and "bad" is that which causes me pain. An individual determines right and wrong based on how these concerns affect them.

For example, the moral content, "It is wrong to steal," is normally supported by reasoning that says, "It is wrong to steal because you can get in trouble if you steal." The main consideration is not concern for others, but only concern for self. What makes stealing wrong is the fact that you could get in trouble for doing it. The only real consideration is the effect upon oneself.

For children striving for survival on the streets, stealing is right because it is the way they get money or food. Prohibitions against stealing have little force for children with no other means of survival. What else can we expect of them when they are left to provide for themselves by their own means? Their moral reasoning is controlled by self-interest, and self-interest says, "Do what you must to survive." As a result, stealing, prostitution, deception and any other behavior that helps a child survive becomes "right" in their minds.

Many adults function at this level for their entire lives. Societies break down if people function only according to self-interest. The adults who abuse street children are also reasoning only in relation to self-interest, believing their actions are "right" because they bring them pleasure. Level one reasoning leads to a continual cycle of people who think only of themselves, never grasping larger issues of "right and wrong."

Level two judgments

Level two morality, called *conventional*, thinks about others as well as oneself. Level two thinking concerns itself with rules and regulations, and wants to obey the law. A person at level two understands that society is more than self, that there are others to consider and that individuals must obey rules and laws for the good of all.

Level two reasoning will explain that stealing is wrong because it is against the law. Stealing is against the civil law of the country, or against God's law in the Bible. Either way, what makes it wrong is that it violates a law.

In its simplest form, this reasoning concerns itself with pleasing others who are important to me. I will not do those things that displease those who are important to me, and I will do those things that please them. Later, this level recognizes that rules and laws are the expressions of those things that please a society.

Yet, those to whom the person is committed control this level of thinking. If the person is trying to please a morally mature person, conventional reasoning can be quite good. Many Christians, for example, are concerned with doing what pleases Jesus. But if the commitment is to a criminal, the behavior will follow accordingly. In the mind of a child, he or she is doing right because it pleases the person to whom the child is committed.

It is normal for children in later childhood or adolescence to move into level two of moral reasoning. The authority for their moral decisions rests outside themselves, and they depend on others to sort out their moral issues for them. Level two is more mature and better than the self-centered reasoning of level one, but it depends on completely external influences.

If those responsible for writing the laws of a society and those responsible for enforcing the laws do not obey the laws themselves, it is practically impossible to expect others to obey them. Sadly, many street children are not protected by the laws or by those responsible to enforce the laws in urban settings. Such conditions keep the children functioning at the lowest levels of moral reasoning.

Level three judgments

Level three reasoning, called *post-conventional*, is concerned with ethical principles. It can judge the rules and regulations of a person or society, and decide if they are in keeping with universal ethical principles. Even if everyone else is doing something, if I judge that something to be naturally wrong, I will not do it. Stealing is wrong because it violates the rights of others.

Level three morality is in touch with the law God has written in our hearts (Romans 2:12-16), and understands that universal ethical principles are more important than self-interest, or even the laws and expectations of a community. Persons who function at level three can look into their own hearts and know right from wrong internally.

The most important ethical principle is *justice*. Level three reasoning seeks the best for all people, and is aware when injustice is being carried out. Above all else, at level three persons make their moral decisions around issues of justice.

The Bible is greatly concerned with justice. Condemnations of people and societies who were unconcerned with matters of justice fill the Old Testament. The opening chapters of Isaiah make this clear. Justice is an issue that is close to the heart of God, and should be close to the hearts of God's people.

All persons begin in the first level of moral judgment. As a child first begins to make moral judgments, these judgments will be made according to the structure of the first level. As moral reasoning begins to mature, the second level will become more controlling. Finally, if moral development continues, thinking will progress to the third level. The levels, however, are always achieved in the same order.

Approaches to moral education

Adults working with street children need to address the matter of morality. But how can these children be taught? Several different approaches have been tried. A brief overview of these might be helpful.

Teaching moral behavior

The most basic approach is concerned with getting children to behave properly. By rewarding good behavior with praise or even prizes, the adult attempts, in effect, to "buy" good behavior from children. This approach is very popular in some forms of public education, and does work to keep children under control. Children will learn to behave in the ways the leader wants, if the rewards are good.

The long-term effects from this method, however, are not strong. If someone with a better set of rewards comes along, the children can be easily led astray. In addition, this approach does nothing to help the child develop any internal moral strength.

There are times when God teaches us in this way. The biblical teachings of obedience leading to blessing and disobedience leading to cursing is clearly a system of rewards and punishments. There can be a place for this approach, but it is limited in its usefulness.

When children have been traumatized and corrupted from their experiences of street life, this may be the place to begin. Rewarding good behavior and ignoring or punishing bad behavior may be the only language of moral education they understand. A careful system of rewards for doing right can be a good starting place to develop the moral understanding of children.

It is much more powerful to reward good behavior than it is to punish bad behavior. Children who have been abused by adults do not need more punishment. Positive rewards will do more than punishments to help correct behavior.

Teaching moral content

A second approach, common in religious groups, is to focus moral education on teaching right from wrong. The teacher has a specific set of beliefs about right and wrong, and so passes on these beliefs to the students. The role of the teacher is to tell the children what is right and wrong.

Teaching moral content recognizes that moral and ethical guidelines exist, and they should be taught to children. There are clear and firm guidelines that children must know. Many children living on the streets have virtually no concept of right and wrong. No one has ever told them, "This is right and this is wrong." Helping children know right from wrong can be very important to their moral development.

A purely content oriented approach, however, does little to change moral behavior. Children can learn right beliefs about moral issues and yet never do them. While it is important to teach moral content, this approach alone is not adequate.

Children from the streets have been in a context where moral absolutes have not been taught. The only absolute they know and understand is survival. Therefore, those who work with these children must help them to learn right from wrong. Teaching moral content, helping children learn right from wrong, will be a critical part of an overall approach to working with street children.

Such basic truths as the Ten Commandments provide guidelines for moral behavior. These need not be taught as rigid laws that must be obeyed to avoid God's punishment. Rather, they can be presented as guidelines for proper behavior so that everyone may benefit. The Bible is an excellent source of basic moral guidelines.

Moral truth is best taught in the context of relationships. Level two reasoning is an extension of relationships, where children want to please others who are important to them. If the adult loves the child, and the child can receive that love, the child will be willing to accept the moral beliefs of the teacher.

Jesus taught this truth when he said "If you love me, you will keep my commandments" (John 14:15). He linked the acceptance of what he taught to his relationship with his students. If children know that an adult loves them, and the adult tells them truths they should believe, children will believe it. The context for teaching moral content is a loving relationship.

The implication for ministry to street children is obvious. Adults who desire to help them must be willing to enter into relationship with the children, earning the right to be heard. There must be a marked difference between how this adult treats the children and how other adults have treated them.

Modeling morality

A third approach to moral education is demonstrating what is expected. Children are very sensitive to the examples set by other people. Moral values are as much "caught" as they are "taught." Children imitate those around them, naturally following the example of others. Moral education must include regular setting of examples for children to follow.

Adults working with street children must "practice what they preach." They must behave in the ways they teach the children to behave. If we want the children to respect the rights of others, we must also respect their rights. We must be willing to live by the moral standards we teach the children. Just as children learn to steal and deceive from the examples of others, so they can learn correct behavior from the examples of others.

The apostle Paul wrote, "What you have learned and received and heard and seen in me, do . . ." (Philippians 4:9). People will do as we do, not just as we say.

The Bible correctly teaches, "Bad company ruins good morals" (1 Corinthians 15:33). If possible, remove children from the influence of the streets. Residential facilities for street children offer the greatest hope for rehabilitating them.

The just moral community

A final approach to moral education is called the "just moral community." This method is especially helpful with people who have little sense of morality, but it is also a very difficult approach to maintain.

A school or institution becomes a community, focused on treating all people with justice. The children will normally be functioning only at level one, thinking almost exclusively about themselves. Such moral reasoning naturally leads to problems, because what is good for one person may not always be good for another.

Teachers lead discussions with the children, helping them discover the problems with thinking only about themselves. Such discussions take time, and must be conducted regularly. The goal is to help children discover that they must consider the rights of others.

As their thinking matures, the group establishes rules of conduct for their community. They become very legalistic as they attempt to establish more and more rules to control their behaviors. They discover that rules and regulations are a necessary part of living, and that rules and laws make things better for everyone.

As the process continues, they discover that they cannot establish rules for every situation. The rules of the community become so detailed and specific that they cease to be of real help. Finally, they discover the principle of justice, treating everyone with equal respect and concern.

Prisons and schools serving very disadvantaged children in the U.S.A. have used this approach successfully. It is time-consuming and difficult to do, but it also has the best long-term results of any approach to moral education.

No single approach to moral education is the best. Each has strengths and weaknesses, and each can be used in combination with others. The key is to understand that we must consider both the "whats" and "whys" of moral issues, and that there is a clear progression of thinking that we can encourage.

The natural order of development of moral thinking is through these three levels of moral judgment. Hearing how children reason about moral questions helps us understand their level of moral reasoning, how we should teach them and how they need to grow.

Guidelines for working with children

There are no guarantees when working with children, especially with children who have been neglected and abused while living on the streets. But the following suggestions can assist us in helping children develop morally.

1. Reward good behavior

Children respond to rewards, especially in the training of moral behavior. Because children reason moral issues first in relation to themselves, it is appropriate to reward correct behavior. Prizes for doing right can be an important first step to moral education. The reward must be something the child values, but it does not have to be costly. Even words of praise from a respected teacher or leader can be an important reward for a needy child.

One useful approach can be the use of a chart or record of good performances. Each time children do right, they receive a star on the chart. When they earn a certain number of stars, they receive a prize. In this way prizes are not given out all the time, but only as a child shows consistently good behavior.

2. Ask "why" questions regarding moral issues

Teachers must not be content to have children give the right answer regarding moral issues. Children must also be able to discuss why a behavior is right or wrong. Teachers must be concerned with structure as well as content in children, seeking to understand the reasoning that is supporting a moral choice. Not only must children know that "stealing is wrong," but they must also be aware of why it is wrong.

As adults work with street children, teaching right from wrong must be accompanied by discussions on why things are right or wrong. Such discussions help the adult avoid the error of being satisfied when the child can give the right answer. Street children have learned to say what adults want them to say. That is part of how they survive. But learning proper moral behavior is more than learning right answers; it is growing in the structures that support the moral decisions. The "whys" are every bit as important as the "whats."

3. Provide opportunities for moral problem solving

Children learn best not from teaching or telling, but from

their own experiences with moral problem solving. As they experience the effects of their choices on themselves and others, and are taught to think about what has happened, they will mature in their moral reasoning. Lectures on moral issues are not particularly powerful for children; but discussions about moral issues and experiences with moral dilemmas help moral growth.

Discussions with children on such topics as, "What happens when we steal from others," help them explore moral problem solving. Helping them discover the consequences of their behaviors, and to explore better answers to their problems helps them grow as moral persons.

If their only possibility of survival on the streets is through stealing, prostitution and violence, children will continue to function at the lowest levels of moral behaviors. Self-interest becomes a matter of survival. Unless we as adults can offer hope of a better way of life, we cannot expect moral growth in the children of the streets. All the discussions in the world will not help if there is no possibility of a better way of life.

4. Treat children with respect

A climate of respect greatly enhances moral development. Adults must respect children as people, listen to them, and speak to them with respect. Because moral development is concerned with justice, an environment where justice prevails makes growth much easier.

Clearly there is a kind of respect reserved for adults. But we must treat even children with respect, because it is in such a climate that they will learn to respect others. Most street children have never been treated respectfully, and therefore have no concept of what it means to respect others. At the heart of morality is respect for the rights of others.

Street children live in situations where they do not have the "luxury" of moral growth. They are literally fighting for their lives, being abused and ignored by the world around them. As they grow into adulthood, they will continue to function outside the norms of society, not having the moral knowledge necessary for civilized behavior. As caring adults, we must intervene on their behalf, feeding, clothing and caring for them. Part of our intervention must be moral education, because ultimately it is an agreed upon set of moral precepts that hold a society together. Moral education is not just a luxury; it is a necessity for modern society.

7

Nurturing physical and mental development

Leah Wenthe

Every year around the world thousands of young people run away from home or become homeless. Despite the large population of such children, little empirical information exists on homeless youth. Most information is based on selected data samples from youth in shelters or institutions. While there is no prototype for homeless youth, research has identified characteristic patterns presented by them that are applicable to street children in most cultures.

Regardless of background, usually a theme of familial discord surfaces in the children's histories. They may have chosen the street to escape physical or sexual abuse or placement in unsuitable group or foster homes. They may be victims of neglect or abandonment. They may have been pushed out of their homes by unwanting parents or because of economic reasons. They may have been orphaned, separated from their homeless family or illegally emigrated without relatives or economic resources. Their families are often dysfunctional in that parental drug and alcohol abuse, poor communication, neglect and violence are likely.

Often through no fault of their own, children are forced onto the streets. Most homeless youth cannot return home. The circumstances that rendered them homeless, combined with the harsh realities of street life, make these youth extremely vulnerable to a host of physical and mental problems. Existing problems that preceded homelessness will likely worsen and lead to other problems.

Moreover, the extent of developmental consequence is directly related to the age of the street child. The younger the individual is when they become homeless, the greater the risk of developmental damage. Research shows that street children are younger today than in previous years and suffer from multiple and more severe problems.

Street life has a variety of negative consequences on the development of children and youth. These include anatomical and neurological defects, health concerns, developmental delays, and psychological and educational problems. This chapter will briefly review factors contributing to physical and mental developmental delays children experience when living on the streets.

Physical consequences

Street youth experience more health problems than the general population. Being homeless aggravates existing medical conditions and increases the prevalence of others. To what extent it jeopardizes physical development depends primarily on the age of the youth. The period ranging from gestation to toddler age is the most critical developmental period and damage that occurs during this time may be irreversible and more significant than damage sustained at other developmental ages. The effects of malnutrition during adolescence, for example, are easily remedied with a balanced diet. Malnutrition of an unborn, however, may cause permanent neurological damage resulting in low birth weight, cognitive deficits and emotional disorders.

Most of the medical conditions that develop during a child's time on the streets are due to an interacting set of environmental conditions and individual predispositions. Incomplete immunizations, poor nutrition and poor hygiene are the major factors contributing to a vicious cycle of poor health.

Incomplete immunizations leave the body susceptible to infection and disease. Poor diets further suppress the body's immune system, leaving the children even more susceptible to disease. In turn, poor hygiene facilitates the rapid spread of infection. The following specify other key causes for health problems among street children.

Malnourishment

Ordinarily common childhood diseases do not affect the physical growth of properly nourished children. In malnourished children, however, these diseases interact with malnourishment. The harmful effects of one contribute to the harmful effects of the other, compounding the consequences. To sum up, incomplete immunizations provoke disease. Disease reduces appetite and limits the absorption of nutrients, causing malnutrition. Malnutrition adversely affects physical development.

As L.E. Berks[1] points out, the fact that immunizations containing live disease agents (e.g., smallpox, polio, diphtheria, tetanus) have virtually no growth impact on well-nourished babies but often lead to significant weight loss in malnourished ones, clearly demontrates the vulnerability of malnourished children to infections. Medical concerns associated with incomplete immunizations include measles, mumps and rubella, polio, diphtheria and tetanus. Left untreated, these disorders impair hearing, muscle development, brain function, vision, breathing, heart function and cause death.

Survival techniques

Lacking resources and little or no income provokes many street youth to engage in risky maneuvers to survive. These survival techniques may also have detrimental effects on their physical health. For example, many, including those with babies, report sleeping in abandoned buildings, vehicles and parks. Aside from being dangerous, these environments are unclean. Respiratory infections, gastrointestinal illnesses and skin disorders are especially common conditions aggravated by unsanitary living conditions.

Prostitution, survival sex and drug sales are other methods street children use to obtain resources. In 1988, one fourth of a sample of homeless youth in New York City reported engaging in survival sex.[2] In the Philippines an estimated 30 percent of Manila's 50,000 to 75,000 street children (both boys and girls) are involved in prostitution. They are among the highest paid of working street children, earning up to US$20 an hour for their services. Similarly, in Thailand, where 40,000 children under age 14 are estimated to be involved in prostitution, the price a brothel owner will pay for a young girl is roughly equal to one year's earnings for a poor Thai farmer.[3] Such survival methods can lead to sexually transmitted diseases, AIDS, pregnancy, violence, substance abuse and death.

Sometimes street children find more legitimate forms of work. Those who get jobs tend to work in hazardous sites such as factories, dumps, sanitation departments or warehouses. Many youth report working in extremely polluted environments with very poor safety standards. Working long hours (up to 15 hours per day) in physically demanding positions for meager wages is commonplace for employed street youth. Whether or not these youth realize how deleterious their actions are is uncertain. Strikingly certain, however, is that these individuals are willing to endure extreme circumstances in order to survive on their own.

Stress

Another agent influencing the physical health of street children is stress. The elements of street life challenge a child's ability to cope. As the duration increases, a youth's coping mechanisms become overwhelmed and produce a chronic state of stress. Chronic stress results from repeated exposure to stressful situations, exposure to very traumatic events or an inability to successfully cope with stress. While studies have shown that small amounts of stress are not harmful, even at times beneficial, chronic stress has been shown to cause adverse physiological reactions. Disruptions of digestion, sleep patterns and sexual activity, increased blood pressure, blood sugar and cholesterol levels, infectious diseases and even cancer are all associated with chronic stress.

Barriers to medical service

Medical treatment for street children is generally unavailable or inadequate. Health care services often fail to reach this population for several reasons. This population, in particular, avoids contact with city resources. All too often the government system fails the children by returning them to abusive households or placing them in unfit group or foster homes. The children generally lack the understanding that they need treatment. Since they have no consistent contact with adults, such as teachers, their problems frequently go unnoticed. Additionally, they have no means to gain access to health providers.

Homeless youth typically have no economic resources available to pay for service. If they receive care from public facilities, they are usually unable to comply with treatment requirements such as bed rest and special diets. When they need prescription medications they cannot afford to fill them or fail to take them correctly. Furthermore, many street children do not comprehend the importance of preventative medicine for proper health maintenance. They are unsupervised children; like all children, they live in the immediate present.

Developmentally, the ability to weigh current behaviors against future consequences is a complex thought process that does not appear before sometime in adolescence. A child's medical knowledge is minimal, often incorrect and lacks insight. For the most part, persistent fevers, dizziness or headaches do not alarm children. Whereas an adult may question the significance of lower abdominal pain and seek medical advice, a child will simply evaluate the pain as a "tummy ache." Fear is another barrier. Like many children, they may be afraid of doctors and thus avoid seeking treatment.

Decreased motivation

Another cause for health problems is decreased motivation. Very often street youth report feeling unloved and worthless with little to live for. They feel dirty or unclean, like "garbage to be thrown away." Why, then, would they attempt to secure good health? Unfortunately, many do not. The combination of all of these factors seriously reduces the likelihood that these children will receive the care they desperately need.

Drug abuse

Most ailments common in street life cause high levels of pain and discomfort. For example, untreated asthma makes breathing unbearable. Some skin rashes or sexually transmitted diseases also produce extreme physical discomfort. Additionally, feeling unloved or abandoned causes mental pain equal to or above those of the physical nature. Given an exorbitant amount of pain, human nature's avoidance of pain plus unavailable health care, we can understand why many street children attempt to self-medicate with alcohol and drugs. These substances are available and effective ways of escaping, however temporarily, the trauma and pain experienced when living on the streets.

The World Health Organization (WHO) reports that one of the most pressing health problems facing the world's street children is the issue of drug abuse. In South America, particularly Colombia, Peru and Bolivia, there has been a tremendous growth in the consumption of cigarettes laced with a low-grade by-product of the cocaine production process. This by-product, known as *basuco*, is especially toxic because it contains kerosene, sulfuric acid and other poisonous chemicals used in extracting cocaine from the coca leaf.

WHO also states limited data suggests that a majority of street children regularly use drugs. In Guatemala, as many as nine out of ten street children are thought to be addicted to paint thinner, cheap glue or more potent drugs. Similarly, in Colombia a 1987 study estimated that 95 to 100 percent of Bogota's 12,000 street children were involved with drug consumption of some kind on a daily basis.[4]

Marijuana use also is frequently reported among homeless youth. Marijuana is a mind-altering drug that affects perception. Over time it, too, can produce negative, long-lasting effects. Smoking marijuana, like cigarettes, can damage the lungs and cause the heart to beat faster and work harder. It has been shown not only to impair memory and physical coordination but also to interfere with normal development.

In females, THC (the active chemical in marijuana) affects the reproductive hormones and may produce lasting effects in the development of the reproductive organs in teens. In males, THC lowers the sperm count, decreases the mobility of sperm and increases the formation of abnormal sperm.

Studies have also shown that marijuana use may reduce the ability of the immune system to protect itself against diseases such as cancer and AIDS. Characteristics associated with marijuana use during adolescence include apathy, indifference, a narrowing of interests and an inability to successfully, maturely, independently and responsibly cope with the adversities of life. Findings from research studies suggest that young drug abusers are at a greater risk of having school-related problems and psychological distress, such as depression, and more likely to engage in dangerous activities such as unprotected sex and crime.

Alcohol

Alcohol is a nervous system depressant that suppresses the body's senses and control systems. It produces a numbing effect which alleviates physical and psychological pain. Only a couple of drinks can reduce discomfort, the control of inhibitions and anxiety. Street children frequently mix alcohol with drugs. This combination adversely affects perception, judgment and reaction time, thereby increasing the risk of accidental death. Excessive substance abuse exposes them to long-term health risks, including diseases of the brain, nervous system, liver, pancreas and heart. It can also cause ulcers, increased blood pressure and malnutrition.

Adverse effects on development

Street life has a variety of adverse effects on the neurological and anatomical development of children and youth. The following describes some of the more critical factors.

Age—a decisive factor

The most important factor for predicting the extent of damage is always the age of the individual at the time of injury. As previously mentioned, the period between gestation and toddler age is critical in terms of developmental growth. Injury during this period can cause dire long-term consequences. Aside from physical abnormalities at birth, developmental damage may become apparent throughout life. For example, early in life developmental milestones such as sitting up and speech may be delayed. Later on, problems in language development or muscle coordination may arise. During adolescence, a child might not develop higher thinking skills such as perspective taking skills, systematic reasoning skills, or the ability for abstract thought or the formulation of hypothesis.

Babies at risk

Given the importance of the period between gestation and toddler age for children's development, perhaps the problem causing the most concern is the rise in pregnant youth. Some young women may have been thrown out of their homes because of pregnancies. Some of these pregnancies result from sexual abuse in the home. Others become pregnant while living on the street. Unprotected sex with multiple partners through prostitution, survival sex, rape and transient relationships increases the likelihood of pregnancies. Although the number of homeless mothers is unknown, its prevalence is noteworthy.

CHILDHOPE reports in a study of 38 street girls in Guatemala that 95 percent have been sexually abused and 21, or 55 percent, had been pregnant at least once. Eight of the 21 said they had had abortions, only one of which was conducted in a hospital or clinic. Eight of the 38 girls also reported having suffered from a sexually transmitted disease.[5]

Unfortunately, most pregnant teens on the street seldom receive proper prenatal care. Unmonitored pregnancies, combined with poor nutrition and dangerous living conditions, can have serious consequences to both the mother and her child. The young mother may develop high blood pressure or diabetes, strokes and birth complications. Aside from the health hazards associated with lacking prenatal care and mental and emotional issues of young motherhood, developmentally speaking, pregnancy itself causes no physical ill effects.[6]

Children born to mothers who have not received adequate prenatal care are at exceptional risk for a range of long- and short-term developmental problems. For example, these children are two to four times more likely to be born with a low birth weight and three times more likely to die within their first year of life.[7] These children are also at higher risk for post-natal growth deficiency, birth defects and abnormalities, irritability and hyperactivity, short attention spans and learning disabilities during school-age years. They are also much more likely than their housed peers to suffer the effects of malnutrition and environmental deprivations.

Not only are the number of pregnant teens increasing, but also homeless families with children are the fastest growing group within the homeless population.[8] Investigators estimate the number of children under the age of six living in New York City shelters to be approximately 6,000, and the number of school-aged homeless children at about 10,000.

Psychological problems

Living on the streets will cause deterioration in the mental well-being of even the most resilient of people. Several risk factors influence whether a particular mental disorder will become manifest itself. When youth who are vulnerable toward a certain disorder are exposed to chronic or acute circumstances, the particular disorder will appear. Street youth experience a variety of traumatic events. How they mentally respond to these events depends on their individual character, the nature of the event and any predisposition they may have toward a mental disorder.

For example, victimization through abuse or neglect leaves many youth vulnerable to depression. Homelessness intensifies feelings of hopelessness and helplessness, thereby increasing the likelihood that the depressed state will become further agitated. Generally, the accumulation of many risk factors increases the likelihood that a particular mental disorder will result.

With that in mind, most researchers have found homeless youth to be at high risk for mental health problems. Consistently, studies have demonstrated high rates of depression, suicidal thinking and suicide attempts among this population.

Depression

Emotion, cognition and motivation are aspects of mental health adversely affected by depression. Emotional symptoms include prolonged sadness, loss of pleasure for enjoying activities, dejection and low self-esteem. Pessimism and hopelessness affect cognition and influence the ability to learn. Boredom and apathy diminish motivation, further reducing the ability to learn and to change harmful behaviors.

Depression produces loss of appetite and energy as well as sleep disturbances which, in turn, have a negative impact on both physical and mental health. Children born to depressed mothers are often deprived of parental affection and stimulation vital for normal development. Particular growth delays are believed to result in children who had mothers with depleted emotional resources, making these mothers emotionally unavailable to meet their children's need for attention.

Suicidal thinking

Street children are particularly susceptible to thoughts of suicide. As I. Weiner[9] suggests, children who come from disrupted households and feel rejected by parents suffer a higher incidence of suicidal tendencies than those children who come from supportive, cohesive homes.

Behavioral disturbances

The prevalence of behavioral disturbances among homeless youth when compared to their housed peers is also significant. In 1984, Citizens Committee for Children sampled eighty-three homeless families in New York.[10] They reported that 66 percent of the mothers noted behavioral changes in their children as a result of homelessness. These changes included an increase in acting out behaviors, fighting, restlessness, moodiness and depression. E. Bassuk and L. Rubin also found a high prevalence of problem behaviors in preschool-age homeless children.[11] Compared to their housed peers, homeless youth in this study had significantly more problems with attention, withdrawal, shyness, sleep, speech and aggression. Among twenty-nine children between six and eleven-years-old assessed for behavioral disturbances, 66 percent of boys and 50 percent of girls indicated a need for psychiatric evaluation.

Intervention

This chapter reveals that street life has a variety of negative consequences on the development of children and youth. These consequences have an impact on every area of human development—from anatomical and neurological to emotional and behavioral to interpersonal and educational—throughout the entire life course. The abolishment of homelessness is ideal. Realistically, however, we not only must develop effective intervention programs but also strategies to prevent its underlying causes. Because there is no single cause for homelessness, intervention must be comprehensive and multifaceted.

NOTES

1   L.E. Berks, *Child Development*, 2nd edition (Needleham Heights, Massachusetts: Allyn & Bacon, 1991).

2   G. Yates, R. Mackenzie, J. Pennbridge and E. Cohen, "A Risk Profile Comparison of Runaway and Non-runaway Youth," in *American Journal of Public Health* (No. 78, 1988), pp. 820-821.

3   From "Fact Sheet on Street Girls" prepared by CHILDHOPE, USA. Taken from *Meeting the Needs of Street Children: Philippine Experience* (Manila: Department of Social Welfare and Development and UNICEF, 1989).

4   Marilyn Rocky, *Street Children and Psychoactive Substance: Innovation and Cooperation*, WHO Programme on Substance Abuse (Geneva, Switzerland: April 18-22, 1994).

5   "Fact Sheet on Street Girls," 1989.

6   L. Steinber, *Adolescence*, 2nd edition (New York: Knopf, 1989).

7   Leah Wenthe, *A Children's Defense Budget* (Washington, D.C.: Children's Defense Fund, 1989).

8   P.D. Kurtz, S.V. Jarvis and G. L. Kurtz, "Problems of Homeless Youth: Empirical Findings and Service Issues," in *National Association of Social Workers*, 3 (4, 1991), pp. 309-314.

9   I. Weiner, "Psychopathology in Adolescence," in *Handbook of Adolescent Psychology*, J. Adelson, ed. (New York: Wiley, 1980).

10 Cited in Y. Rafferty, "Developmental and Educational Consequences of Homelessness on Chldren and Youth, " in *Homeless Children and Youth: A New American Dilemma*, J. H. Kryder-Koe, L.M. Salamon and J.M. Molnar, eds. (New Brunswick, New Jersey: Transaction, 1991), pp. 105-139.

11 E. Bassuk and L. Rubin, "Homeless Children: A Neglected Population," in *American Journal of Orthopsychiatry*, 57 (2, 1987), pp. 279-286.

PART THREE:

Other Intervention Concerns

8

Confronting drug and substance abuse

Jeff Anderson

Drug and substance abuse is strongly associated with life on the street. Drug use presents one of the most pressing health problems facing the world's millions of street children. For many youth worldwide, drug use represents a form of adolescent experimentation and rebellion. For street children, however, drug use offers an escape from the harsh daily realities of family break-up, poverty, abuse and homelessness.

While it is widely acknowledged that drugs are a symptom of street life, drugs do not necessarily send children to the street. Drugs, however, are widely available to the children when they become a part of the street environment.

During a presentation at the international conference of the American Public Health Association, Mark Connolly[1] cautioned the audience to ". . . take into account that street kids do not see drugs as part of the problem. They see drugs as a part of the solution—a coping mechanism." Drugs become a means of escape and release from the daily pressures of street life and survival.

Street children's reasons for their drug use

Marilyn Rocky[2] cites the following reasons given by street children for taking drugs:

◆ We take drugs to have the confidence to beat others and have adequate courage to steal.

◆ You take drugs so that when you get caught stealing and get beaten you will not feel the pain.

◆ To forget problems and become happy.

◆ Drugs give you ideas for finding money.

◆ To help you sleep.

◆ Drugs help you so you don't feel pain.

◆ It makes you more courageous, so that you fight someone when they refuse to pay for your services (reported by a girl involved in prostitution).

◆ So that if you have to kill someone, you don't see it as a bad thing.

◆ So that when you are stealing you don't feel shame.

◆ So you don't think.

◆ When you are chased by your mother.

◆ Sometimes you are accused of using [drugs] when you don't, so you decide to use them.

Other reasons children report for using drugs include family problems and conflicts, fights or problems with girlfriends or boyfriends, fighting off cold or hunger, keeping awake for work, keep alert to possible violence, to get to sleep, to numb physical or emotional pain, to replace the need for food, and peer pressure.

Although use of drugs by street children is functional in most situations, they increase health risks and may lead to high levels of exploitation and violence. Some children also—either voluntarily or under pressure—become involved with the manufacture, traffic, distribution and sale of drugs. For others, drugs may provide status within the street community, especially when they are involved in the various phases of trafficking in drugs. In some areas access to services and protection are linked to compliance with drug traffickers.

Kinds of drugs and substances used

Most street children in developing countries use drugs that are most readily available and cheap. For example, glue in areas where shoemaking is common, solvents in industrial areas, coca paste and cocaine in coca producing regions, opium or heroin in opium producing regions.

Various forms of inhalants (industrial glue, paint thinner, nail polish remover) are almost universally used as is alcohol, nicotine, cannabis and pharmaceutical products. The younger children mostly sniff glue and paint thinners, while the teenagers consume alcohol and smoke marijuana, which is sold cheaply in the lower-income suburbs.

Many of the more expensive drugs are available to children on the streets. Whether they use them or not usually depends on their contacts and their means and source of income. Street workers need to become familiar with these drugs and the effects they have on the children.

Three categories of drug involvement

People who work with street children will confront three different groups of children involved in the world of drugs: the user, the abuser and the addict. The worker must not mistakenly treat the user as an addict nor should the addict be treated as a user. Though sometimes slight, there is a difference between drug use, drug abuse and drug addiction. It is important to know where one type of drug involvement begins and ends and where the next type starts.

The following comparisons may help: think of the drug user as a social drinker, the drug addict as an alcoholic and the drug abuser as a problem drinker. The drug user uses the drug, but the drug uses the drug addict. The user can control the amount of drugs she takes but the addict cannot control herself or the drug. The user is an experimenter, the abuser is someone who finds he has an ever-increasing need to experience the high or the euphoria it gives him; the addict is someone who seeks total escape from reality.

Addiction defined

Addiction has been defined as a state of periodic or chronic intoxication produced by the repeated consumption of a drug and involves tolerance, psychological dependence, usually physical dependence and an overwhelming compulsion to continue using the drug which detrimentally affects both the individual and society.[3] The World Health Organization (WHO) recommended replacing the term "addiction" with a single and more general term: "drug dependence." WHO describes drug dependence as "a state arising from repeated administration of a drug on a periodic or continuous basis."[4]

Most abused drugs and their effects

This section details the drugs frequently used by street children, along with descriptions of their side effects.

Alcohol

In small doses alcohol has a tranquilizing effect; a person may feel relaxed and free from tension, although alcohol can act as a stimulant in some people. In larger amounts alcohol depresses brain activity, and may temporarily impair muscular coordination, memory and judgment. More intake over a short period can result in loss of control and dulling of the senses. Continuation of steady heavy drinking can anesthetize the brain and result in a coma or death.

Used in moderation, alcohol apparently does no permanent harm to the body. Taken in larger quantities over long periods of time, it can damage the liver, brain and heart. It can also result in permanent brain damage so that memory, judgment and learning ability deteriorate.

Marijuana or "hash" and "hash oil"

Marijuana is smoked, sniffed and ingested. The active mind-affecting ingredient in all three forms of this drug is THC. The flowering tops and leaves of the marijuana plant contain the highest THC concentration. Hashish or hash is a dark brown resin from the top of the plants. It is much stronger than crude marijuana because it contains more THC. "Hash oil" is a distillate of the marijuana plant with a concentration of THC even higher than hash. The effects on the user are more intense and the possibility of side effects is greater.

The effects of marijuana vary so widely that it can be considered either a stimulant or a depressant. THC is often considered a hallucinogen with some sedative properties. Some users are talkative, giggle, or act silly, while others become boisterous, moody and drowsy.

Marijuana does not lead to physical dependence but some users may become psychologically dependent on it. The psychological effects of marijuana are quite variable. Thoughts may be dream-like; users often report illusions, misinterpretations or sensations. But hallucinations and delusions are rare except at very high dosages.

Amphetamines or "speed"

Amphetamines and methamphetamine are stimulants, and are often called "uppers" or "speed." The most common stimulants used on the streets are white cross (pill), meth tabs (pill) and crystal meth (powder). Methamphetamine hydrochloride is the most abused illegal drug in the Philippines, where it is called *shabu*.

The street abuser will take excessive amounts of speed for long periods of time. Such a person is drug dependent. Some abusers inject massive doses of speed once or up to a dozen times a day. This kind of use can cause sudden death.

Speed produces a euphoric high which decreases over a few hours. When the effects wear off, the user feels depressed and sluggish. Taking more speed relieves these symptoms; however, larger doses become necessary to produce the same effects. This cycle can go on for days until the person is physically exhausted. Shakiness, itching, muscle pains and tension are common. Collapse and death have occurred.

Many people who use speed also neglect their bodies in various ways. Kidney failure, hepatitis, drastic weight loss, malnutrition and infection from the use of unsterile needles are some of the physical hazards.

A person who uses large amounts of speed becomes overactive, irritable, suspicious and often becomes violent. A condition resembling paranoid schizophrenia, with severe delusions of persecution and hallucinations, often occurs.

Barbiturates or "downers"

Barbiturates are often called "barbs" or "downers." Barbiturates are sedatives used to reduce anxiety and excitement. They also are used to treat medical problems such as high

97

blood pressure and peptic ulcers. They fall into the category of major tranquilizers.

"Downers" on the street are sometimes used by heroin users either to supplement the heroin or to substitute for it if heroin is not available. People who take speed sometimes use "downers" to offset the jittery feelings it produces.

"Downers" can cause physical dependence. Taking large doses produces a strong desire and need to continue taking the drug. As tolerance to the effects of barbiturates develops, a user needs more of the drug to get the same effect. Withdrawal symptoms also occur when one stops taking the drug. Withdrawal symptoms from large amounts of barbiturates are usually much more severe than withdrawal symptoms from heroin.

Usually a person who has taken large amounts of barbiturates goes into a coma. If a user is tolerant to large amounts of the drug, they may stay awake but appear intoxicated. Speech and movement may be uncoordinated and judgment and perception impaired. Accidental deaths may occur when a user takes an unintended larger or repeated dose of barbiturates because of confusion or impairment in judgment caused by the initial intake of the drugs.

Alcohol and barbiturates taken together may be fatal since the dangers of one are increased by the other. Many accidental deaths have been blamed on a mixture of sleeping pills and alcohol. Barbiturates and barbiturate-like drugs (such as methaqualone), when taken with narcotics or anesthetics, may also cause extreme, sometimes fatal reactions.

PCP or "Angel Dust"

PCP or phencyclidine was developed in the late 1950s as a human anesthetic. Because many patients developed adverse side effects, its use was discontinued. Currently it is produced and regulated for veterinary purposes only, primarily as an anesthetic for large animals.

As a street drug, PCP first appeared in 1967 on the streets of San Francisco. Because PCP can be easily manufactured in illegal laboratories, it became easily obtainable and its use spread rapidly. The effects of PCP vary greatly with dosage and with the way it is used. PCP can be taken orally, sniffed, smoked or injected.

Most adverse reactions occur with large doses, although they can occur at any dose level. After taking an average dose, a user may begin feeling the drug's effects within 15 to 30 minutes. The individual becomes noncommunicative and reports being in a state of oblivion and fantasy. This high can last from four to six hours during which the user may become very talkative. Gradually the individual falls into a state of mild depression, becomes irritable, feels isolated and sometimes frightened. After 24 to 48 hours the user generally returns to normal. This average dose response can be positive for some but extremely unpleasant and frightening for others.

Since dosage is so variable and uncontrolled, more bizarre reactions are common. Feelings of depersonalization and weightlessness are commonly reported along with perception distortions, extreme feelings of apathy, indifference, estrangement and emotional and social isolation. A person may become irrational, belligerent, violent and assaultive. Other effects of PCP are continued impairment of concentration, learning and memory functions, reaction time, sensory discrimination and physical coordination. High-dose states are often seen in emergency rooms and deaths from overdoses have occurred.

Cocaine

Cocaine is a drug derived from the coca bush found in some South American countries. Injected or inhaled, cocaine produces over-alertness, euphoria and a feeling of great power. The high is much like that of a large dose of speed except that cocaine is very short-acting.

Researchers do not agree on whether tolerance to cocaine develops but strong psychological dependence does result. As with speed, depression occurs when the drug's effects wear off. This depression is "cured" temporarily by the use of more cocaine, thereby contributing to the development of a cocaine habit. Heavy cocaine use will lead to weight loss, sleeplessness and anxiety. Paranoid delusions and hallucinations often occur with heavy use.

LSD

Lysergic acid comes from a fungus and was first converted to lysergic acid diethylamide (LSD) in 1938. Nearly all LSD comes from illegal laboratories or is smuggled internationally. The quality of the drug varies. Some LSD is fairly pure. Most street LSD, however, contains impurities. Generally the user has no way of knowing the purity of LSD or any other drug obtained on the street.

LSD is a hallucinogen. This drug affects sensation, thinking, self-awareness and emotions. Changes in time and space perception, delusions and hallucinations may be mild or overwhelming depending on the dose and the quality of the drug. Effects vary and the person may have different reactions on different occasions.

During an LSD "trip" a person loses control over his or her normal thought processes. Although many reactions are pleasant, many perceptions may cause panic or may make a person believe that he cannot be harmed. Both of these reactions may bring about behavior that can be dangerous to the user. Longer term harmful reactions include anxiety and depression or "breaks in reality" that may last a few days to several months.

The exact cause-and-effect relationship between LSD use and emotional disruption is not known. When a person has suffered from emotional disturbance before using LSD, the drug may simply trigger an emotional breakdown. "Flashbacks" can also occur. A flashback is simply a recurrence of some feature of an LSD experience days or months after the last dose.

Mescaline

Mescaline comes from the peyote cactus and has effects similar to LSD. Mescaline is also categorized as a hallucinogen.

Narcotics

Narcotics include opium and drugs derived from opium such as morphine, codeine and heroin. Narcotics also include certain synthetic chemicals that have a morphine-like action such as Demerol and methadone.

The life expectancy of a heroin addict is significantly lower than that of an individual who uses other drugs. An overdose can result in death. If, for example, an addict obtains pure heroin and is not tolerant of the dose, the addict may die within minutes of injecting it. Infections from unsterile solutions, syringes and needles cause many diseases. Serum hepati-

100

tis is common. Skin abscesses, inflammation of the veins and congestion of the lungs occur.

Glue and paint thinner

In Manila and other cities around the world an increasing problem among poor children is the sniffing of chemicals—especially rubber cement glue, paint thinner or solvent, shoe polish, gasoline and cleaning fluid. Workers see children with a plastic bag full of glue or a rag doused in solvent almost always held up to their noses. When inhaled, industrial glue produces light-headedness, occasional hallucinations, loss of appetite and nausea.

These products are readily available at any hardware store and are sold to street children even though the store clerk knows this product will be used for getting high. I have even met solvent pushers on the streets. When I asked one boy why he sniffs glue he told me it was "like heaven" and he did not feel hungry. Somehow the miserable plight of street children helped me understand what he meant.

Multiple drug use

Multiple drug use is very common. People who use one kind of drug are more likely to use other kinds of drugs as well—either by taking various drugs in sequence or at the same time. Greater risks exist when a combination of drugs or a mixture of unidentified pills are taken. This is especially true of alcohol and barbiturates.

Physical implications

Children use drugs because they get a sense of euphoria and a distortion of their senses. The side effects of regular drug use, however, can have serious physical implications.

Because street children are difficult to track for follow-up study, there is very limited data available to substantiate all the long-term health problems associated with their drug use. Nevertheless, evidence suggests that the impact on the children's long-term health include lung damage, irreversible brain and kidney damage, malnourishment and a general weakening of their health. A constant need for escape from extreme poverty and hunger through drugs leads a few to insanity by the time they are in their early twenties.

Counseling the drug user

Drug use serves as both a "high" and a temporary escape for children. The pleasure may help the children's feelings but eventually can destroy their lives. Drug users must be made to see that they are escaping from—not coping with—life. They are using drugs to hide from life's seeming unbearable realities and trials rather than facing them head-on.

The counseling process

The counseling process must address and seek solutions to the root causes that have led children into drug use. The more children and youth turn away from—rather than toward—life and its challenges, the more they get used to escaping and so continue their need for more drugs.

Children also need to be told the facts about what drugs will do to them physically and mentally. They need to hear and understand the darker side of drug use—the damaging effects beyond the "high." Usually they think that they will never become hooked on drugs. But once drugs go into the body and mind, will power and reason, good sense and sound judgment all disappear.

Another danger is that a person does not know just how they will react to a drug. For example, reactions to the use of marijuana can be different. The initial effect is often nil. First-time smokers usually get sick while some report no effects after several uses. Eventually, however, the user will begin to experience a mild sensation and perhaps get "stoned." The effects come on slowly and smoothly. After repeated use, if the dosage happens to be stronger, the effect can be frightening.

If children can be made to see the long-term effects of drug use including loss of values, distortion of character, weakness of personality and physical and mental deterioration, then they may be able to understand that their drug use has an adverse effect on their total being. Only then will they be ready for help and change.

Drug dependency as a means of coping leads to drug abuse. Drug users never intend to become abusers. But slowly and subtly the process takes place. Before they know it, it happens. And when it does, it is a blow to their egos and a frank revelation to themselves that there is something wrong with them. This shattering revelation usually means they need more drugs to alleviate the pain of this knowledge.

Drug abusers are in the process of becoming addicted. Most likely they will not see their involvement in drugs as a serous problem. Users and abusers see only the "high" side of drug consumption. Often abusers are at a phase of their drug-taking cycle where they derive satisfaction, euphoria and release of tension from the chemical they are using. They feel no pain.

What can a counselor offer?

What can you as a counselor offer drug abusers? The symptoms are pleasant and the cure is painful. The low side of drug use—the side effects that bring misery and suffering—may not yet have appeared. Therefore, it is difficult for drug abusers to be motivated enough to examine their reasons for using drugs.

Abusers usually withdraw and will not come out of their seclusion unless the counselor makes contact with them. The counselor's greatest task is to make contact and keep contact alive. From this contact the counselor can work with the abuser until the counselor-counselee relationship develops. Users and abusers are saying "Please help me!" with their drug-taking. But they do not know they are saying this. Not until they understand that drugs do not give answers, but instead destroy, will they be ready to accept help.

Usually the problems caused by drug-taking prepare the person for rehabilitation: criminal arrest, sickness, physical weariness, family and home conflict, jail and hospital confinement, social stigma, the merry-go-round of hustling for the money to support drug habits. Apart from the above reasons, addicts usually do not want help.

Rarely will drug abusers submit to counsel or rehabilitation in the early stages of their drug use or addiction cycle. The addict views her drug use as a cure and not as a problem. If the addict is on mind-expansion drugs, she will have a feeling of superiority and wisdom. Not until an addict has had a few bad trips (they do come eventually) and not until she suffers the related miseries of addiction, will she be a good candidate for counsel and rehabilitation. Therefore, do not play the "ready or not, here I come" game with the addict.

What can you do for the user, abuser or addict who has not been motivated to seek help? In some cases you can do nothing but wait for the situation to get worse. When it does, you may be able to help that person. The challenge and task of the counselor will be to watch and wait.

You must, however, keep the lines of communication open. Through the counselor's Christian witness, addicts may recognize their spiritual need and seek help. Through an experience with Christ, their dependence on drugs will be alleviated. Bible promises such as "I came that they may have life, and have it abundantly" (John 10:10b) are powerful promises for addicts to rely on.

It is difficult to counsel the addict while he is under the influence of drugs. The opposite condition is when the addict has not had any drugs for a period of time and is suffering withdrawal. In his time of need, the withdrawal period may be an excellent time to reach the addict. In his pain and suffering, he can be led to look to God for help and strength. Without drugs to depend on, the issue is forced. He has to do something to get through the withdrawal. He usually does one of two things: he either runs away from or toward God.

Whether children are drug users, drug abusers or drug addicts, they can experience freedom from the bondage of drugs. Their only true freedom, however, lies in a totally changed life, which only Jesus Christ can accomplish for them.

[Appreciation and acknowledgment for much of this material goes to Midwest Challenge, a Christ-centered drug and alcohol rehabilitation center located in Minneapolis, Minnesota, U.S.A., and their manual *Wisdom from the Street*. I worked with them from 1977-1984. Much of my current work with street children in the Philippines is based on what I learned or experienced while serving with Midwest Challenge.]

NOTES

1   Marilyn Rocky, "The Role of International NGOs in Relation to Street Children and Substance Abuse," in *Street Children and Psychoactive Substance: Innovation and Cooperation*

(Geneva: WHO Programme on Substance Abuse, April 18-22, 1994), p. 5.

2   Ibid.

3   *Wisdom from the Street: How to Rescue Your Kids Before Someone Else Has to* (Midwest Challenge, Inc., 3049 Columbus Ave. South, Minneapolis, MN 55407 U.S.A., 1976), p. D-24.

4.   Ibid.

9

Preventing and treating HIV and STDs

Eric Ram

Contributing factors to the problem

Youth is generally a time of robust health. Continued life on city streets, however, poses a number of health threats on an almost daily basis which, in time, grinds down even the most resilient of children. Perhaps the most daunting health threats are AIDS (acquired immunodeficiency syndrome) and sexually transmitted diseases (STDs). (AIDS is a disease caused by the human immunodeficiency virus [HIV].) Unplanned teenage pregnancies among street children, without prenatal care, also poses a threat to the health of both the mothers and the children.

High-risk environment

Street children become sexually active at a very early age. Emotionally vulnerable and economically poor, these children are easily drawn into selling sexual favors. In many parts of the world the prospects of protection against STDs and HIV are next to nil for child prostitutes of eight, nine and ten years of age. For most of these destitute children, hard drugs are far beyond their means, so their biggest risk of contracting STDs and HIV comes from sex.

Many have run away from sexual abuse at home only to face more abuse from older boys and adults on the streets. Some are at risk of STDs and HIV infection through sexual relationships they form—for a variety of reasons—with other youngsters on the streets. Many children sell themselves just to survive. For others, sex provides the emotional comfort they so desperately seek.

Children forced into the streets are faced with the pre-existing conditions that favor the spread of HIV/AIDS: a high prevalence of other sexually transmitted diseases and unprotected sex, shared needles among intravenous drug users, ignorance, lack of information, nonexistence of health and social services, violence, fear of police, sense of hopelessness, ostracism, stigma and shame.

The frequency of sexual encounters and the multiplicity of sexual partners make street children particularly vulnerable to HIV infections.

Substance abuse

Given the nature of the problems street children face, coupled with the hardships they confront once they are on their own, it is no wonder that so many of them try to numb their pain with drugs and alcohol. Often the children are forced to sell their bodies for sex to support their drug habits, which further exposes them to a number of communicable diseases, including STDs and AIDS.

Not only do these children experience the immediate consequences of their drug use, but for many the drug culture and the economy associated with it become an integral part of their lives.

Street girls

Once on the streets, girls often form peer groups or gangs, similar to their male counterparts. They also form surrogate families with common-law husbands who serve as their protectors. Girls are often in competition with each other for boyfriends and clients, which often leads to violence. The most common problems faced by girls on the street are sexual abuse, prostitution, unwanted pregnancies, unsafe abortions, STDs including HIV/AIDS, poor nutrition, respiratory infections, skin diseases, drug abuse and abuse by police. They also suffer from psychological damage, which manifests itself in aggressive and violent behavior, depression, violent withdrawal and self-mutilation.

Invariably girls complain that they have no place to go for their health needs. If they do manage to find a health clinic, they often receive second-rate treatment by health care providers unless they are accompanied by someone from an organization that provides assistance to street children. Access to medical care and health services for street children is generally considered inadequate for a variety of reasons: scarcity of services, fear of health professionals, legal difficulties at treatment facilities, lack of confidentiality, the behavior of the children themselves and the lack of interest and inability of health promoters and service providers to deal with these children.

Street girls who are sexually active are at much greater risk of contracting STDs and HIV. Illness, injury and death also result from early pregnancy and childbirth.

Demand for younger sex partners

The HIV/AIDS pandemic has a direct effect on young lives, having created a greater demand for young sex partners in many countries. The market for sexually exploited children and youth involved in prostitution is growing rapidly because clients believe that younger children are less likely to have AIDS.

Today a tourist in Europe, Australia or Japan can buy the services of a young boy or girl at the same time as he pays for his hotel and return flight. This practice has been going on for twenty years or so, but recently the trade has become more organized. Not only are the children exploited, they are also exposed to the risk of contracting STDs and HIV. Usually the infected adults pass the infection on to unsuspecting youngsters, who are generally ignorant of the risks involved.

The tragic reality is that sex between an adult and a youngster is more likely to result in the transmission of STDs and HIV to the youngster rather than the other way around. Girls are especially vulnerable to STDs and HIV infection because the thin blood tissues lining a young girl's vagina are easily ruptured and torn during sex with an adult male, giving the HIV virus a direct passage to the bloodstream.

The girl being prostituted by several men a day ends up with internal injuries such as bleeding and abrasions, which never really have a chance to heal. Once infected with STDs and HIV, young girls have a greater possibility of sexually transmitting the infection to their partners. Thus, sexually exploited children become both receivers and transmitters of STDs and HIV.

AIDS orphans

According to the World Health Organization's (WHO) Global Program on AIDS, at least 1.5 million of the world's children today are orphans because one or both of their parents have died of AIDS. By the year 2000, according to conservative estimates, this number is expected to zoom to the 10 million mark. Susan Hunter, a UNICEF consultant, accepts an even worse scenario; she says there may be as many as 28 million AIDS orphans in the world by the end of the century.

But why count the orphans? To emphasize that the number of AIDS orphans is only going to get bigger in the foreseeable future, and that more children are going to be pushed onto the streets. In the past, when the number of orphans was small, extended family structures served as an effective safety net for the orphans in a community. Now that the orphans are many this safety net is developing some very large holes.

The reasons for these holes include: 1) heavy migrations from rural areas to big cities and towns, which have weakened old family ties; 2) booming population growth that has put enormous pressure on limited agricultural and land resources, making it more difficult for families to provide food, shelter, clothes, health care and education for the children; and 3) the deaths of both parents in thousands of nuclear families. This last factor has turned an already bad situation into a desperate one.

In many cases, we are seeing uncles and aunts who earlier accepted orphans into their homes now dying or seriously ill from AIDS. In many communities in the developing world, the few healthy adults are already trying to care for more orphaned nieces and nephews than they can reasonably manage. More and more grandparents are now the only adults to care for their grandchildren, and children of 11 or 12 years of age are often the only caregivers for their junior siblings. AIDS has stretched countless extended families to their limits and robbed thousands of children of their childhood.

The impact on a child of the loss of a parent has psychological, physical, economic, social, spiritual and legal implications. In addition, AIDS orphans are forced to leave school and look after the remaining family members. These children, who are completely unprepared for their new role, are generally abused and rejected. Many respond to these pressures and responsibilities by trying their luck in the cities, where they are likely to join the growing number of street children, many of whom are already infected with STDs and HIV.

The manager of World Vision's Rakai program in Uganda tells the tale of a twelve-year-old boy. The boy says he will never return to his family home just a mile away where his brothers and sisters still live; he cannot bear to see the grave of his much-loved father.

He tells, too, of an eleven-year-old and a seven-year-old who experienced the death of both parents from AIDS, and then the death of their grandparents who had taken over the children's care. The two children decided to walk to their mother's village 150 kilometers away to look for their relatives. They got as far as World Vision's office 30 kilometers away before they were stopped. "It was sheer desperation," the World Vision manager said. "They didn't know where or to whom they were going; they just felt there must be someone out there to call 'mother.'"

The psychological state of such children is a matter of concern, but there is no clear understanding of the issue. People working with AIDS orphans in Uganda admit that this is an area of expertise which is particularly lacking in their programs. "We have real difficulty getting kids to tell us how they feel," said the World Vision program manager. "But there are many signs. When children sing, they sing of AIDS, and they sing and cry. In Luwero they used to sing about war. In peaceful places they sing of nature. But here they sing of 'Slim' [another name for AIDS]."

The cost of HIV/AIDS on orphans is inestimable in terms of death, suffering and negative development. It has both direct and indirect costs for the society.

Stopping the increase of AIDS orphans will mean teaching mothers and fathers how to avoid acquiring HIV. In Kenya, World Vision projects in Korogocho, Kiberia, Rwiru and Loitokitok are doing just that. Using traditional styles of storytelling, songs, dance and drama, project workers are teaching the local herbalists and midwives about proper HIV/AIDS prevention and care. To stop HIV/AIDS, we are going to need such creativity in many areas.

Preventing AIDS and STDs

In general more unprotected premarital sexual relations are taking place at earlier ages, giving rise to the increased problems of too-early pregnancy and childbearing, induced abortion in hazardous and risky circumstances, STDs and HIV. According to WHO studies, STDs among young people have increased markedly in the past 20 years and are among the most common causes of illnesses.

The presence of STDs in general and genital ulcers in particular provide a fertile ground for easily contracting AIDS. Most common STDs are gonorrhea, syphilis and chancroid. The list of complications associated with STDs has grown considerably during the past ten years: sequelae of pelvic inflammatory diseases, genital cancers, infection of newborn babies and infants, narrowing of the urethra and infertility in men. These have severe psychological effects on children because of their unpredictability and the risk of infecting others. Presently, genital herpes and HIV/AIDS are not curable.

Because street children are growing and are in a period of profound physical and psychological change and experimentation, their risk-taking behaviors such as unprotected sex, sharing needles for injecting drugs, and injury due to violence render them very vulnerable to HIV infection.

Abstinence

The best way to prevent children from getting STDs and HIV is abstinence from sexual intercourse or an exclusive sexual relationship between two partners who are free from STDs and HIV. Given the way of life on the streets, however, this solution is easier said than done. The next best thing is for the children to protect themselves by using a condom during sexual intercourse and not sharing needles with others for injecting drugs. Not injecting drugs is best, but if they do, then using sterile injecting equipment is the next best alternative.

STDs can be prevented and treated. HIV can be prevented but cannot be treated. In all cases information on how diseases are contracted, how they can be prevented, how they are diagnosed and how they may be treated must be given to children. Governments and NGOs (nongovernmental organizations) must also make counseling and clinical services available to the children.

Street children to street children

Young people generally are suspicious of adults and are more open to accepting advice from their peers. From many experiences around the world, such as the street educator program, workers have learned that peer education programs can help street children. These programs increase the children's knowledge, skill and behavior regarding their sexual development and practice, reduce their risk of contracting STDs and HIV, prevent unwanted pregnancy and minimize health risks.

Peer education can help children's contemporaries realize the potential risks of their sexual behavior and educate them in how to protect themselves. It also encourages children to think about their values and the consequences of their decisions, and helps them build confidence. Because children prefer to learn about sex from their peers, the peers have to be adequately informed and educated on sexual activities and prevention.

Street children should be involved early in the formation of children-to-children peer groups so they feel the plan is for them and came about on their own initiative. Children have other priorities, of course, which workers must take into consideration.

Young people must choose their own criteria for and method of the selection of peer street educators. Because they are young and inexperienced, they may need some adult guidance and advice, given in a non-threatening way. Some projects offer to pay street peer educators their expenses for travel and meals. In other projects peer educators are responsible for managing the small budgets needed to run various activities.

As much as possible, efforts should be made to arrange for peer leaders to meet and talk with individuals who have HIV/AIDS. This approach helps them to understand that the exercise is not just theoretical; real people like themselves are vulnerable to HIV. They can then communicate their experience to other young people. If they are willing, some HIV-positive persons can also be trained as street peer educators.

GPA/AIDS Action reports that participatory training methods are usually the best methods for exploring attitudes and developing skills while also being stimulative and enjoyable. Since young people learn quickly, their greatest need is for help in building their trust and confidence in working with groups. The street peer educators also need to feel confident about who they can contact for help, support and guidance.

Providing help and care

Early diagnosis and treatment of AIDS and STDs in children exposed to sexual abuse are very important because the infection may be asymptomatic. An STD that remains untreated may result in unanticipated complications at a later stage and may be transmitted to others. Young people's ignorance of the symptoms of STDs, their reluctance to ask for help, the lack of health care or clinics and the fact that many STDs may remain inside the body without showing obvious symptoms are some of the main problems in the control and treatment of STDs.

We can—and must—take action to eliminate the basic causes that push children into the streets. We must provide care, hope and love so that perhaps one day there will be no more deprived children living on the streets.

Practical actions

NGOs are in a unique position to do a number of things for street children. They can identify needs and gaps in services and provide these directly to the children. For example, make primary health care available to street children by encouraging them to take advantage of this service. Train street educators to encourage the children to learn. Have workers act as advocates for the children in the challenges they face. Provide skills and vocational training to help children support themselves. Develop holistic programs that aim at managing drug abuse.

A primary goal must be to help improve community attitudes toward and understanding of street children, thus helping to reduce the likelihood of discrimination against them. Enlist former street children to help rescue those currently caught in the relentless cycle of street life. Take preventative steps to reach out to thousands of would-be street children before they take up residence in the streets. Groups can join forces and resources in the fight to keep drugs off the streets. Provide safe havens for these children today so they may have a better chance for a more productive future.

Compassionate care

Street children are in need of many things, but love and hope are two of the most critical needs. These children live in constant fear of many things, and these fears need to be replaced by love, compassion and hope. Since they live in despair much of the time, they turn easily to various sources from which they can draw strength and hope. Some receive fundamental needs through their peers, some through counseling, some through the gangs they belong to but very few through spiritual beliefs. To them God may seem a very distant reality as they struggle for survival on a daily basis. Yet, I believe that we, as Christian health professionals, can help in several ways:

- ◆ We can pray with them as we care for their physical and psychological needs. The former is needed but would have little effect without the latter.
- ◆ Show them that compassion is more than pity and sympathy by exhibiting that we have the capacity to feel their pain and suffer with them.
- ◆ We must be willing to experience something of the reality of street life: its fears, isolation, anger, frustration, loneliness, anxieties, violence, its assault on the childhood of a young person, the loss of dignity, the utter vulnerability, the risks and the alienation.

Children respond to love and compassion more than to threat and punishment. Compassion enables healing to reconstruct the child. Children may never recover their lost child-hoods, but they can experience a sense of wholeness within despite everything around them. The task is not easy by any means.

Most street children programs tend to concentrate on the children's physical needs. These are essential, but not their only needs. We also must heal the attacks on the spirit just as we do the attacks on the body. When STDs and HIV/AIDS attack the body, they also attack a person's mind and spirit because body, mind and spirit are inseparable. Compassionate care also means that although many street children cannot be fully reha-bilitated or adequately cared for, they can still experience inner healing.

The responsibility for compassionate caring is not limited only to health care professionals or social workers, but must also be shared by every member of the community. If we care for our children with compassion at home, they would proba-bly not end up on the streets. This may be the most cost effec-tive preventive measure. Compassionate care also compels us to treat children with respect which, in turn, restores their dig-nity.

Let us not prevent the children, especially the street chil-dren, from coming to Jesus Christ, as Jesus' disciples attempted to do. For Jesus said: "Let the children come to me, do not hin-der them; for to such belongs the kingdom of God" (Mark 10:14b). Then he placed his hands on them and blessed them.

We adults have a strong tendency to pass judgment on young people. We even blame them for losing values. How-ever, Kingdom values are applicable to all. Preventing conflicts and wars, alleviating poverty, maintaining family harmony and preventing STDs and AIDS are adult responsibilities for which we cannot blame the children. Adults also have the responsi-bility to guarantee that children are not deprived of their child-hood. We must love our children unconditionally, just as the Lord Jesus Christ loves them.

REFERENCES

AIDS Action. June-August 1994. "Young People First," in *Appropriate Health Resources & Technologies*. Action Group: London.

Blake, Dorothy. "Social Aspects of HIV/AIDS and Children," in *Children Worldwide*, ICCB 20: No 2-3/93, Geneva.

Baldo, Mariella. 1993. "Preventing HIV Transmission Among Teenagers and Young Adults," in *Global AIDS News*, GPA/WHO.

Gutman, Laura T. et al. "Human Immunodefiency Virus Transmission by Child Sexual Abuse," Dept. of Pediatrics, Duke University Medical Center. A paper presented at the annual meeting of the Society for Pediatric Research, Anaheim, California, U.S.A., May 1990.

KIT *AIDS Health Promotion Exchange*. 1994. KIT, The Netherlands.

Ram, Eric R. Oct.-Dec. 1994. "Health Risks faced by Street Children," in *Together*, World Vision International.

Nouwen, Henri. 1979. *The Wounded Healer: Ministry in Contemporary Society*. Garden City, New York: Doubleday and Company Inc.

UNICEF. 1990. *Children and AIDS: An Impending Calamity*. New York: UNICEF.

WHO. 3-7 Feb. 1992. *Street Children Project Report of Inaugural Meeting of Participating Centers*. Geneva: World Health Organization.

WHO. 20 March 1992. *World AIDS Briefing*. Geneva: World Health Organization.

WHO. 1993. *The Health of Young People: A Challenge and Promise*. Geneva: World Health Organization.

WHO. 1994. *AIDS: Images of the Epidemic*. Geneva: World Health Organization.

PART FOUR:

Responding to the Children's Needs

10

Street worker profile

Jeff Anderson

What are the requirements for becoming a worker among street children? Matthew 9:35-37 and James 1:27 indicate a street worker primarily needs a calling, a motivation and a God-given burden to reach street children. The ministry needs and the children require long-term, committed workers who are willing to work together as a team.

A calling

To be an effective worker with street children, an individual must first have a personal calling from God. Such a calling will enable workers to persevere, even when things get difficult. Workers must be spiritually, mentally and physically strong in order to engage the city and the city's poor.

A worker who has been especially called by God, also has the ability to love the people they are called to and develop a love for the city itself. Called ones will not perceive the children only as souls to be saved, but as persons in need of love and care.

Motivation

A priority requirement for workers is to examine their motivation for working with street children. Having feelings of pity is not enough; pity will run dry very quickly. A worker must have the compassion of Christ, which causes a person to move from an emotional response to an active response.

Workers also must form biblical attitudes toward their ministry and the poor. The attitude and presentation of street workers are vitally important for effective ministry. The primary obstacle to successful programs often is due to a worker's attitude.

Sharing the burden

Becoming "team players" in ministry rather than "lone rangers" also is a must requirement. There are times when someone may need to pioneer a work in an area and be left with no choice but to work alone. But, as in any ministry, the highest goal is to have a team.

Team members contribute a variety of spiritual gifts to a ministry. They also provide fellowship and protection—both physical and spiritual. There is an intense spiritual warfare being waged for these children, a warfare that requires workers to be undergirded with a strong foundation of prayer support and a knowledge of the Word. A ministry team also makes evaluation possible and ensures that more effective work will be accomplished.

Tasks of the street worker

According to Adie Punzelon,[1] a street worker or street educator, is someone who reaches out in ministry to children who make the streets their home. When holistic ministry is the goal, the interventions offered will be multifaceted.

Know your target audience and their needs

Street educators first need to identify their target audience—the street children who are in need of assistance. Once you have identified these children, assess their needs and understand clearly the problems they confront. At this point, a worker is ready to plan intervention strategies.

Also workers now are in a position to present their requests to groups that have resources, or to coordinate efforts with other agencies or churches. The street educator is a vital link between agencies, churches and the street children.

The street educator also can be a vital link between the child and the community law enforcers. Often children are not aware of the rules that communities have concerning their presence or work in a particular area. As a result, they can be unaware of having broken any laws.

Immerse yourself in the children's world

Street workers must frequent places where the children gather or congregate. You need to observe the times children meet and repeatedly make your presence felt during those times. This strategy has two purposes: first, it provides opportunities to become familiar with the people in the neighborhood, the children and the their environment; and, second, it makes your presence part of the children's visual field. Make this an ongoing strategy.

Identify with the children

Make it a point to smile at every child you meet. Do not expect them to smile back, but keep doing so yourself—it will make their world a little brighter, and yours, too. And don't be afraid to approach the children; it is acceptable to greet them with a cheery "hello."

Just as you are getting to know the children, they, too, will be getting to know you. Street children do not trust strangers immediately. If you put on an authoritarian air, they may feel threatened and be suspicious of your motives. Once trust is established, you can begin to know the children better, discovering what they think and believe about themselves.

Wear simple clothes and avoid wearing make-up, jewelry and uniforms. If possible, wear your house clothes; children will identify with you more easily. You can communicate that you are part of their environment through your appearance.

When talking to children, try to be physically equal with them. If possible, sit down and maintain an eye-level posture while conversing with them. Look the child in the eyes but do not expect him or her to do the same. It is normal for a street child to avoid your gaze. As they start to feel at ease and develop trust in you, however, their gaze will become steady.

Know the language of the children. They develop their own terms for places, people and events—and especially danger signals. By knowing their slang, you will get to know them better, understand how they perceive things and how they sur-

121

vive. Speaking their language makes it is easier for you to enter their inner world.

Memorize the name of each child. Know the kinds of work they do and the games they play. Try to join in on these activities. If they are scavengers, join them in one of their sorties; if they push carts, accompany them and discover what it is like to push carts. If they are playing hide-and-seek, volunteer to be "it."

Try to avoid giving money to the children. When they ask, try to find out what they need it for. If it is really urgent, like helping someone who is sick, try to take the sick person to a health facility. If a child is hungry, buy food instead of giving money.

When a child touches you, do not wipe the touch away; this would be perceived as an insult. Instead, try to reciprocate the touch of the children. Your touch will make them feel loved. Street children have a greater need for cuddling than most children as they usually do not experience this at home. When visiting their quarters, do not cover your nose, even if the place smells bad.

Refrain from sermonizing, especially during the initial stages of interacting with street children. Draw from the children their ideas of what they consider to be good or bad.

When the children start to talk about their problems, listen attentively. Ask open-ended questions—questions they cannot answer with a "yes" or "no." You will be rewarded with more details about their situations and needs. Avoid probing questions.

Cultivate acceptable relationships

According to a survey of street children, they like a street educator who:

- ◆ is a loving, flexible friend;
- ◆ is a source of encouragement, inspiration and protection;
- ◆ gives immediate services and help;
- ◆ knows self-defense and teaches the children how to defend themselves; and
- ◆ plays with the children, helps them with their work and finds time to be with them.

Children are also quick to point out that they dislike a street educator who makes promises but does not keep them—such as not showing up as promised—or one who constantly preaches and moralizes, always finding fault in everything they do. And, again, the worker's attitudes are important to the children. The children are upset when a worker can see nothing but their filth, smell and how dirty they are, never trying to understand them as people, let alone attempting to understand their culture.

Develop an acceptable approach

Children receiving help on the streets report that they prefer a non-threatening and sincere approach (not coming on strong or probing, questioning or investigating their activities). Being relevant in meeting the children's needs is crucial, too. They want protection from the police and other sources of harassment, food and encouragement in what they do well.

Children also prefer an outreach center that is relevant to their needs. This includes having the center located near their work so they can attend school or other activities in their free time. Since many need opportunities for earning an income, they appreciate it when the center can provide income-generating opportunities.

They prefer a simply furnished facility, one they do not need to worry about getting dirty or breaking valuable items. Adequate space is a much appreciated "luxury," especially when children spend most of their time in cramped, overcrowded conditions.

Good food is another strong magnet to draw children into centers for assistance. Many children are hungry most of the time. They do not, however, like it when the staff is served better food.

Provide education

Street education encompasses the educational process that takes place on the street. Through this process, street children receive the opportunity to learn, understand, appreciate and relate to themselves and to others. It is education that teaches children to reflect on their situations and to act on what they can become, thus achieving authentic human development.

123

Make home visits

Ask permission from the children when you want to communicate with their parents or visit in their home. This is a sign of respect for the children.

Validate the information that the child provides by comparing it with that given by the parents. Often a child gives incorrect information on the family, not because he or she is trying to be dishonest, but because of problems stemming from psychological needs.

Children sometimes paint a horrible picture of their families to solicit sympathy. There are those who claim they are orphans when they are not. Many children, because of their early experiences, even "murder" their parents in their thoughts.

Introduce yourself courteously to the parents. Do not display an air of authority or create an impression that you are blaming the parents for the plight of their children. They, too, are often victims of poverty.

If the parents are busy doing something or are working, do not pull them away from their activities. Just talk briefly to them, state your work, tell how you met their child and request to speak to them at a time when it is convenient for them.

After the first visit, always make a follow-up visit. During these visits you can become more personal, carrying the conversation from the superficial toward the real or essential issues.

During home visits avoid promising parents any material or financial help. And do not blame them for the plight of their children or sermonize on their behavior. It is far better to make yourself an example of moral behavior rather than to preach about it. Offer advice only when it is solicited.

Workers also need to be careful that they are not carried away by the emotions of a parent. If parents begin to cry, let them, but try to keep yourself calm so that you can direct the conversation.

Follow-up home visits

After you have won the confidence and trust of the parents, gradually convince them to meet with other parents in the area. Start a sharing group among them to discuss simple issues concerning the plight of street children. Again, do not create the

124

impression that you are blaming them. Your main concern at this point is to raise their consciousness regarding their own and their children's needs. Once they have become more aware of these needs, they will be more adept in analyzing their situations and in exploring ways to respond positively to them.

Families of street children are highly mobile; they move frequently from one area to another. This mobility makes follow-up work difficult. One way of maintaining contact with the children is to establish a network of volunteers who will be on the lookout for new faces in their area. These volunteers should be part of a central coordinating group on the movement of families. This probably is workable only in relatively small areas.

Keep a journal

Jot down your successes and failures in a journal. Mistakes are good tools for growth. The practice of writing down your thoughts will enhance the quality of your reflection process and will better equip you to share effectively with other street educators, workers and organizers.

NOTE

1   Material in this chapter was presented in the Philippines by Adic Punzelon at an Urban Street Ministry fellowship seminar on June 18, 1994.

11

Street addiction can be broken

Helen Shedd

Persuading children to leave the streets should be easy. "Promise them a warm bed, food and some toys and they gladly will leave," people advise. Those who have worked with street children and tried these tactics have found that the solution is not quite that simple.

The focus of this chapter is to answer two questions: Why is it important for children to leave the streets? and, How can workers convince children to leave the streets? The author will address the forceful pull of street addiction and give some suggestions that will help children accept reintegration into society.

Advantages of leaving the streets

There are diverse opinions concerning the most conducive venue for working with street children. The following specifies important reasons why children should be rehabilitated in venues off the street.

Stability

The first, and probably most important, reason why street children must leave the streets for effective rehabilitation to

126

occur is because the street is a completely uncontrolled environment. Children attending outreach programs on the street come when and how they please. Workers have no way of making them come consistently.

In a group home, however, workers can provide a stable environment. A schedule can be established and followed on a daily basis, allowing the children to know what is expected of them. The children have opportunities to learn the meaning of discipline and responsibility.

Stability is important for the workers, too. They must be able to control what is done and when it is done. Whether or not the children will show up ceases to be a major problem in a stable environment. Stability also permits sequential teaching and involvement in long-term projects.

A family setting

Within a group home, a child may be required to behave according to certain guidelines. On the street such a requirement is next to impossible to enforce. By definition street life describes a lifestyle having no guidelines, authority figures or discipline. In a group home one can set up realistic rules and enforce them. Rules provide emotional security for the children, even though initially they may resist them.

One of the greatest advantages of early participation in a group home is that it provides a "family setting" that the child may never have experienced before and which they cannot experience on the street. More than any other force, the love of Jesus that the houseparents demonstrate will compel street children to leave their former life behind. With this in mind, the ministry should make an effort to have the group home function as a family.

If possible, a group home should be run by a couple. When a couple is not available, male and female role models are highly recommended. In order to encourage a family atmosphere, the group home should have a maximum of ten kids. Ideally meals should be eaten together at one table.

Removal from temptations

Working with children in a setting other than the street removes them from many sources of temptation that the streets afford. Drugs, alcohol, prostitutes, as well as the thrill of adven-

127

ture and the opportunity to make easy money, beckon children in a powerful way.

Street children will go through periods of wanting help desperately and will even demonstrate an interest in leaving the street. Those phases, however, may be short-lived and if the children remain on the street they will probably be persuaded to do the things they have always done. Separation from the street and its temptations enhances the likelihood of their dealing with their addictions. Trying to rehabilitate children on the street may be likened to compelling an alcoholic to give up alcohol while living in a pub.

Provision of safety

Safety concerns for the workers and the children are another problem encountered in street-based ministries. On the street, workers cannot prevent the children from becoming high on glue, which causes the children to act unreasonably. Workers also have to contend with the children's companions, who are not always interested in being rehabilitated but rather in distracting or getting in the way. Often these "friends" will use peer pressure and threats to discourage a street child from considering leaving the street or even be seen with an outreach worker.

Other sources of danger on the streets are the pimps and drug lords who "use" the children for their own financial gain. If these abusers feel they are losing money because of the interference of street workers, they may become disruptive and even violent. If children are taken to a group home, however, they may be dealt with individually without threats to their physical safety.

Besides the safety of the children, there is the mental and emotional state of the workers to consider. Working directly on the street is highly stressful, and an individual has to contend with many dangers all the time.

As already mentioned, there are dangers from the pimps and drug dealers and the children who become violent when high on glue. Often the police become antagonistic toward anyone who is trying to help the children. Some street workers have been beaten before they have been given an opportunity to explain their real intentions. All these dangers put an enormous amount of stress on the worker.

On the positive side, ministry workers are often privi-leged to witness God's miraculous protection. This author observed a completely drugged youth furiously lunge toward a worker. As the youth's fist approached the worker's face, it stopped in midair and was lowered in slow motion. The drug addict tried to lunge a second time; once again he had to lower his fist in slow motion. He was not able to even touch the worker.

Barriers to leaving the streets

There are many reasons why it is difficult to persuade children to leave the street and receive the help they so desper-ately need and often desire. Some of these reasons are listed below. You will have to address these issues in your interven-tion planning.

Street addiction

When making a decision to give up street life, a major obstacle confronting the children is street addiction. This addic-tion is powerful, widespread and one of the most difficult to relinquish. The street offers the children a life of complete irre-sponsibility. Street children believe they are completely free to do what they want when they feel like doing it.[1]

When the children are hungry, they steal to buy the food that they desire at that moment. When they see tennis shoes or designer clothing they want, they find ways to steal them. Many street children believe it is ridiculous to work hard for a meager salary that is not sufficient to buy the things they desire.

In order to understand street addiction, you must realize that for many children, coming to the streets has been a long process. Many come from abusive home situations, or situa-tions of abandonment or severe poverty. In Brazil, many are victims of abuse by their stepfathers.[2]

Many children begin their escapades on the streets by beg-ging or trying to earn money by performing simple tasks such as shoe shining, watching cars or selling small items. Others are on the streets to spend time with friends, escaping difficult sit-uations at home. On the streets, children discover others expe-riencing the same plight. These peers can sympathize with them and, over time, become "family."

In the initial "romantic period" life on the streets is new, fun and highly adventuresome; the children still have family contact, display some respect for their families and often go home to sleep at night. This is the time children who are considered to be "on" the street are most receptive to receiving help.

Once children have broken all ties with their families and no longer return home, they are known as children "of" the street. Children of the street are the most difficult to reach. After they have passed the romantic phase, however, and they face the disillusionment and sorrow of street life, some again become softened and open to change.

Distrust of people

Distrust of people is a major stumbling block that prevents children from leaving the streets. In the past, many of the children were badly treated by adults they should have been able to trust. Now they fear letting down their guard. They often suspect that a worker may be from the police, the juvenile court or social welfare—someone who "takes away those who [do] not have a father and mother."[3]

Even more terrifying to the children is the possibility that the worker may be collecting information about them to pass on to those who take the extermination of street children into their own hands. The children have reason to be afraid; violence toward street children is growing worldwide.

According to a recent investigation by the Brazilian Congress, in the past three years 4,611 children—3,781 of them black—were murdered in Brazil; the rate continues to rise. At least three children a day are killed and others disappear without a trace. In October 1990 a common grave containing the bodies of 560 children was discovered in a Sao Paulo cemetery.[4]

Street children need time to develop trust. The more positive contact they have with a worker, the more willing they become to incur risk.[5] This means that workers must plan activities on the street that enable them to develop friendships with children who desire change.

Demonic activity and influence

A less openly discussed reason for the children's resistance to assistance programs is the demonic activity and influ-

130

ence in their lives. Many street children, especially those in countries where voodoo and spiritism are commonly practiced, were offered to evil spirits before they were born. In Brazil, special blood rites performed by pregnant mothers are often children's initiation into the occult.

Hopes for holistic rehabilitation means dealing with the demonic influences in the lives of street children. The first step is to help the children to recognize and confess the particulars of their past involvement in the occult. Many have made their own pacts and commitments to Satan and some even wear symbolic jewelry or clothing. In Brazil, one of the most commonly used symbols of the occult is black and red beaded necklaces.

The power of Satan in the children's lives is real. A twelve-year-old girl in Sao Paulo, who had been through ceremonies of dedication to evil spirits, was so strong that she nearly broke the fingers of a worker. Thus those who desire freedom from Satan's grip must verbally confess in detail any pacts made with Satan.

Often, setting a child free from demonic influence takes time. Do not become discouraged if the process is slow, but be aware of the powerful hold that Satan has on many children's lives. You must see prayer as a priority in ministry. The struggle between Satan's and God's control in the children's lives is blatant.

Fatalistic approach to life

Many children do not have the will to improve their lot in life or even to survive. They hold to a fatalistic approach that asks, "What difference does it make if we live or die?" Making the effort to change is more than the children want to deal with. They live concerned only with day-to-day survival. Alan Pieratt says:

> People who live on the streets have, as a rule, very low self-esteem, and over time it develops into a deeply set fatalism. They do not believe they are of any value to God or man, and as they grow into adulthood, they begin to believe it is their destiny to live the way they do. They find it hard to believe that God would care for them or that their lives could change for the better. Breaking through

131

STREET CHILDREN

with the gospel requires that the good news of Christ be brought to them time and again in a patient and loving way.[6]

Loss of hope also contributes to the children's fatalistic attitude; often they can perceive no way for things to become better for them.

Program obstacles

Rehabilitating street children is a process. Initially, make contacts and cultivate friendships while the children are still on the street. Then children need a short-term "breaking in" period in a specialized group home or, when necessary, a drug rehabilitation center. Finally, once the children have reached emotional stability and a certain level of personal responsibility, they may be referred to a program offering a long-term solution. The solution could be a return to the family of origin, placement in a foster home, an adoption or assignment to a long-term group home.

The short-term program in which a street child initially becomes involved must be carefully planned and administered. If the program proves to be a disastrous experience for a child, he or she may not be willing to try that, or any other program, again.

Although many programs have aimed to rehabilitate street children, they often have not been successful. The following details some obstacles that may block a program's success.

Inadequate facilities

Some programs become too extensive, attempting to care for far more children than is practical. Such poor planning often results in inadequate facilities and an insufficient number of workers. For effective rehabilitation, children must have adequate space to live and sufficient personnel for their care. Squeezing children into bedrooms packed with bunk beds limits play areas.

A facility's lack of upkeep and supervision often are obvious through such things as broken toys, lack of necessary furnishings or lack of program structure. Children reason that if their surroundings are not important to the adults, they, too,

132

probably are not important. In such a situation, it is not possible to effectively meet the children's felt needs.

Worker motivation

Another obstacle can be the workers' motivation—some are there only for the job. They do not have any true interest in the children's welfare. Such motivation often leads to negative and sometimes violent, rather than loving, treatment of the children. In Brazil, street children often voice their fear of being taken to institutions. One evening last August, a group of children in Copacabana played a rough game in which one boy wrapped a thick rope around the other children's necks, taunting them that they were "being taken to FUNABEM" (the National Foundation for the Welfare of Minors).[7]

The fact is, these children are not always easy to deal with and many will push workers to the limit to see if they will still be accepted. Usually, however, their belligerence toward authority is a cover-up for feelings that stem from a lack of self worth and the inability to do things "properly." Such feelings of hopelessness cause many children in institutions to attempt suicide.[8]

Lack of rule enforcement

Usually it is more difficult to bring about obedience through loving discipline than to just let the children do as they please. It requires great patience to invest the necessary time to make sure the children are being obedient. When this investment is not made, it results in workers either letting the children "run wild" (be undisciplined) or keeping order through violent means.

Open programs

Some workers try to attract street children by having "open programs" in which the children can use the program's facilities whenever they please. Usually places where the children can wash their clothes, take showers, play games or engage in new kinds of social interactions are provided; nothing is required of them. This type of program means that the children miss out on discipline—one of the key elements of rehabilitation.

The children are used to living for the present moment, the present pleasure. With these types of programs, they do not learn the value of work or the discipline of putting responsibility before pleasure. In some ways these programs have a negative effect on rehabilitation. When children leave an "open program" to enter a more serious one, they continue to expect life to be comfortable and easy. In a sense they have been inoculated against true rehabilitation. For this reason, programs conducted on the street (such as street schools), should have set times for the children's arrival and departure.

Lack of positive change

The most serious flaw in many programs is that they are not designed to bring about positive change in the children's lives; their goals are achieved simply by getting the children off the streets. No steps are taken (or opportunities given) for the children to develop spiritually, educationally, vocationally or emotionally.

Programs that attract

Having examined elements of programs that are obstacles to attracting children to leave the streets, let us now examine the kinds of programs that motivate and attract children.

Exciting

To grab the children's attention, programs must sound exciting and be equipped to meet the children's needs. The children must be assured that they are not going to be locked up in a room all day as if they are in a juvenile detention center. Instead, opportunities will be provided for them to run and play, to study and do chores.

Plan plenty of activity into the schedule. If a program does not have good recreational facilities, research the recreational options available in the community. You may be able to use the local park's swimming pool or the community's outdoor game facilities.

Provides dignity

An important characteristic of an attractive program for street children is that it imparts a sense of dignity. A program with some kind of vocational training is ideal for imparting dignity and self worth. Depending on the program's resources, the children may be trained in marketable skills such as iron-smithing, wood joinery, silk-screening, cement block-making,

134

tile-making, flower arranging, candy-making, tricot-knitting, crocheting, sachet-making, embroidery, small-animal raising, vegetable gardening or agriculture.[9]

Other possibilities for skill training include sewing, shoe shining, working a printing press or tailoring. Younger children can make simple arts and crafts that may be sold—collages, macrame, papier maché, basket weaving and so forth.

A program that includes this kind of training, especially if the children are given a small portion of the profit, instills a deep sense of self-realization in a child.

Spiritual nurture

A true conversion experience is essential if children are to be completely freed from the desire to return to the street. There are many ways to provide spiritual nurture, including singing (which most children love), prayer, Bible stories, debates, drama and Christian videos.

Spiritual nurturing will take place naturally and informally if the workers are growing Christians. In many ministries, however, workers are so overburdened that their focus is on doing the task rather than being in a right relationship with God.

Often workers must assume so many responsibilities that they cannot keep up. Soon they become overworked and spiritually drained. When planning an intervention program, it is crucial to schedule adequate rest time for the workers along with opportunities for their spiritual nurture.

Spiritual mentors may be assigned to workers, regular devotional periods planned, retreats and corporate prayer meetings conducted or, occasionally, special speakers invited to talk and share. Workers who are alive spiritually will have many opportunities to demonstrate to the children that there is a God who loves them deeply and will never abandon them.

Love

Love is probably the most attractive feature of any program for street children. According to 1 Corinthians 13, no matter how great the sacrifices in ministry, without love they are worthless. Not only are they worthless before God, but also before the children. The children can sense who does and who does not love them. Damun Gracenin reminds us that, "They [street children] are strongly attuned to adults' attitudes toward them and will reward genuine efforts to establish rapport."[10]

The Bible teaches that love transforms. It should be a ministry's goal to accept only workers who express a call of love to work with street children. Resist the urge to accept workers who are only great fund raisers or fantastic in public relations.

Family oriented

Besides craving love, most street children have a strong desire to belong. On the streets, the children fulfill this desire by banding together in "families" or "gangs." It is natural for them to value a program that resembles a family to which they can truly belong and function as a member.

The home where the program is located should be cheery and tastefully decorated. The decor and furniture contribute to the children's feelings of self-worth. The furnishings, however, should not be of such high value that the children do not feel free to enjoy them.

Structure and discipline are crucial for the development of responsibility in children. A family-like situation can provide both. Discipline should remain on a positive scale as much as possible, rewarding those who behave appropriately. Some programs have successfully adopted point systems. With their accumulated points, children may "purchase" candy or other small items: pencils, pens, crayons or stickers. Those who prefer to accumulate points over a period of time may purchase T-shirts, tote bags or other nice prizes.

Choice of location

Those planning to encourage children to leave the streets should choose program sites as far removed from city streets as possible. From the author's perspective, the ideal place for a program is out in the country. This distances the children from many sources of temptation. It also makes running away on a bad day more difficult.

Another advantage of being in the country is cheaper and more available land, meaning that a program can usually afford to have more space in which the children can run and play. Also in the country valuable practical skills such as gardening and raising chickens can be taught. Finally, the chances of old friends coming around to cause havoc is not as likely in the countryside.

It must be noted that it is entirely possible to run a successful program in the city. It is recommended, however, that the ministry establish its short-term intervention home as far as possible from the location where the street children are being contacted. Although temptations will still confront the children, a location away from the city will lessen the influence of their street companions.

What if the children do not want to leave?

In this chapter I have argued that street children should leave the street for rehabilitation. This raises the question, "What if the children do not want to leave the streets?" The fact is, there are some who do not care to leave and never will. There are others who claim to want to leave but as soon as they are put into a program they run away, claiming they do not want to lose their freedom.

Workers should not become discouraged by such responses. For some children, now is not the time for rehabilitation. They are still too thrilled with the adventure of street life. The day will come, however, when they realize that the excitement is not worth the sorrow. For others, that day may never come; perhaps they have made the decision to reject God and life. Some of the most hardened street children, however, are the ones God miraculously changes.

As your ministry makes decisions concerning which children to invest in, seek wisdom from the Holy Spirit. The ministry's goals should include the invitation, opportunity and necessary provisions for children who truly want to leave the streets. The children, however, must recognize their own need to leave the streets and enter a program; they cannot be coerced into doing so.

Because the needs are so great, a ministry should make a sincere effort to concentrate time and effort on children who are serious about change. One fact that concerns many street workers is motivation. "Why is this child saying that he wants to leave the street? Is he or she merely trying to escape a sticky situation with the police?" You cannot judge a child's motives.

137

Some children who enter a program for one reason may end up staying for another.

One way to screen those who say they want to abandon street life is to set up appointments with them over a period of days and observe if they keep the appointments. Those who truly desire to change will take seriously their commitments to the worker.

Summary

Street children need to grow and develop before they can return to their homes and face the situations that sent them to the street in the first place. Some need an opportunity to learn skills that will enable them to earn a living.

To overcome street addiction, it is crucial to have an intensive program in a group home where children may be given a taste of healthy family living, a taste that includes healing doses of structure, love, responsibility and discipline.

Such programs also serve to weed out children who are not interested in genuine change, but rather in a convenient place to eat and sleep with no responsibilities attached. Christian ministries should focus attention on children who demonstrate that they are serious about the life-changing experiences God can bring about in their lives.

NOTES

1   Mac Margolis, "Shattered on the Streets," in *Scholastic Update* (February 12, 1993), pp. 11-14.

2   Flor Romero, "Children of the Streets," in *UNESCO Courier* (October 1991), pp. 16-19.

3   Hartmut Gunter, "Interviewing Street Children in a Brazilian City," in *The Journal of Social Psychology* (132:1991), p. 136.

4   Paul Jeffrey, "Targeted for Death: Brazil's Street Children," in *The Christian Century* (132:1992), pp. 359-368.

5   Gunter, p. 367.

6   Alan Pieratt, "Jesus Loves the Children," in *Impact* (June 16, 1991), p.13.

7   Michaela Jarvis, "No Direction Home," in *Image* (June 16, 1991), pp. 13-19.

8   Ibid., p. 19.

9   Ron Wilson, "Brazil's War on Children," in *World Vision* (February/March 1992), pp. 2-6.

10   Damun Gracenin, "Reaching and Teaching the Homeless," in *Education Digest* (59:1994), p. 38.

12

Starting a ministry with street children

Jeff Anderson

The needs of street children are so immense that starting a ministry for them requires a far-reaching, sustainable vision: a vision that encompasses the scope of our highest goals, a vision so big only God can make it a reality. From that vision, it is vital to lay a strong foundation for ministry-building. This chapter addresses issues concerning ministry vision and ministry development.

Ministry vision

Although the problems of street children are complicated and enormous, with God's help we can catch a vision which will enable us to initiate effective ministries for street children. Without a vision, however, we will become overwhelmed by the magnitude of their problems and needs before we even get started.

As you talk to street children, observe their situations and encounter what they confront on a daily basis, the Holy Spirit will create compassion in your heart for them. Information creates understanding which, consequently, reduces our fears and increases our motivation to respond to the children's obvious needs.

A ministry must be the vision of an entire church or project team, not just the pastor's or a lone worker's. The church must eventually, under the direction of the Holy Spirit, embrace and own the ministry if it is to survive. There can be no life-changing ministry without first catching a shared vision.

Defining vision

Vision is a mental picture that enables a person to understand what God wants to accomplish. It provides an inward and invisible reason for the ministry God is leading you to commence. Vision changes our strategies and plans, enabling us to plan effectively and wisely for the future.[1]

Vision also drives us to action. The only way a vision becomes a reality is for each individual on the team to turn that corporately-owned vision into action in his or her own sphere of influence. To accomplish this, vision must have a practical and detailed plan or strategy whereby it can be nourished and bear fruit. The following are some vital elements that can nourish a vision.

- Commitment: The Word of God and prayer must empower our lives. Through these means we come to know what God desires, and we commit our lives to God's plan.
- Courage: Courage is derived from the security of knowing that our convictions are valid.
- Integrity: We discover integrity in using our place of influence to give to others instead of receiving from others. We need to honor our subordinates, promote our equals and give to everyone credit where credit is due.
- Discernment: Discernment is a spiritual "sixth sense" that comes from walking close to God and staying alert to events occurring around us. We need to be astute observers of people and events; we must be generous and loving but never gullible.
- Perseverance: We need to be prepared to endure opposition and to have a "stick-to-it" mindset. Only those who have risked much in a project can rejoice much in its com-

pletion. Though our fight is not with flesh and blood, it still is a very real fight.

Ministry planning

The worksheets at the end of the chapter will help you plan your ministry. The questions on the sheets will guide you through such crucial tasks as defining your ministry; understanding the children in your target area and evaluating their needs; choosing program methods; and knowing your resources, including the gifts and talents of the workers who will be involved in your work.

Being an integral part of the planning process generates a feeling of ownership of a project or ministry. Project members must embrace the vision if they are to become actively involved in the project's development. Every opportunity offered workers for input, prayer, planning and sharing of information helps build a sense of ownership. No one on a ministry team is an outside critic of the ministry.[2]

Ministry development

> *"Any enterprise is built by wise planning, becomes strong through common sense, and profits wonderfully by keeping abreast of the facts." Proverbs 24:3, 4 (LB)*

Aristotle taught that "why?" is the most important question we can ask. If we cannot adequately answer "why?" we likely cannot answer other questions. "Why?" is the launching pad for anyone contemplating a ministry to change the children's situation.[3]

A purpose or mission statement

A mission statement informs the agenda for the development of a ministry. When we form a purpose or mission statement we express in words and formalize our answer to the question "Why?" Formulating a purpose statement helps answer questions concerning goals, available resources, the children's needs and how best to respond to them.

Research

Research is the place to begin in developing a purpose statement. Research also helps you acquire practical, usable

142

information for developing appropriate programs that address the specific needs of street children in a particular area.

Volunteers concerned for the children in a specific area should initiate and conduct the research. Research will reveal if others are currently working, or desiring to work, among that particular group of children. If no workers are found, then the information can be used to raise an awareness of the situation in that community.

For your particular research, have the team form a list of objectives. There are three sources they will especially want to target for exploration: the church, the community and the street children. These sources will yield information that will enable the team to effectively construct their basis of ministry.

The purpose for doing research on the church, community and children is to develop an accurate profile of needs and resources. Research into these sources will answer the following questions:

◆ Why is this ministry necessary?
◆ Who will do it?
◆ When will we do it?
◆ Where will we do it?
◆ How will we do it?

It is a fact that our resources of time, money and personnel are limited. Jesus exhorts us to count the cost before beginning a project (Luke 14:28-33). Research is counting the cost, lest we foolishly begin a project we cannot complete.

Church

Investigate church resources that may be used for ministry: time, personnel, materials and services. Are there buildings or classrooms that you can use for meetings, classes or counseling? Are gymnasium or youth club (recreational) facilities available? Is the church ready to start a work with street children?

Community

Inquire into the resources of your community from government officials, community leaders, businesses, police, social service agencies and others. Acquire information on what other groups are doing and what they view as unmet needs. Are they involved in preventative, crisis intervention or rehabilitation programs for the children?

Observe the programs of various groups and evaluate their effectiveness in meeting the needs of street children. Establish links with these groups for future networking; they can prove to be useful contacts as your ministry develops.

Street children

A street educator has much to learn from street children; life in the streets is the children's best teacher. The children's environment is full of real life illustrations for instructing them—and you.

Meet the children and start building a relationship of trust with them. Strive to really know and understand them: learn their names, schedules, educational attainments, desires and dreams, sources of livelihood, family backgrounds and felt needs.

Ask the children to describe their idea of a group. If they join one, what would their expectations be? Usually they will cite practical things like money, food, clothing or protection. Let them verbalize their needs; you can sift through their responses later. Make a mental note of their deeper problems.[4]

Organize the children into a discussion group to serve as a vehicle for the expression of their problems and the exploration of solutions. Children who have been in the streets often come up with simple and practical ideas regarding their needs.

Interaction with the children while working on small projects can be a fruitful research tool. Plan projects that bear immediate results. As the children see something concrete from their collective efforts, they will be encouraged to start other activities.

Always complete an activity with a collective reflection session where each child is given an opportunity to share an insight from what was experienced. Encourage the children to listen attentively to one another. If a child makes a particularly enlightening statement praise him or her, but make it a point to comment on each child's insight.

Respond immediately to urgent needs that arise in the groups, like giving food to a hungry child, treating a wound, settling a fight or sending a child to a health center. Doing this with the children will help them value the importance of collective action.

Integrate value clarification exercises[5] into your activities, especially in simple games. Keep a daily record of your experiences. Note what the children say and their reflections concerning situations. Later you can use these insights to emphasize certain lessons.

In every activity, a natural leader normally emerges. Observe those with natural leadership abilities and plan to develop their skills.

Processing the data

After conducting the research the team will need to:

- ◆ evaluate the data;
- ◆ document the data (an ongoing process that you need to perform regularly throughout your ministry);
- ◆ develop program strategies;
- ◆ secure resources;
- ◆ begin the project; and
- ◆ report the results (include photos).

Accountability

When the leaders develop goals, they should factor in accountability guidelines for team members—including the leaders. Team membership means responsibility as well as privilege. Define clearly how the team's performance will be regularly evaluated.

Just as members of a team have a right to expect competent leadership, so the leaders have a right to expect each member to attend meetings, contribute their best efforts and serve the team, the church and the children. Members' failures and successes should be discussed and critiqued in helpful ways that result in growth and development.

Accountability brings structure and discipline, which strengthens the ministry for the rigors that it will face eventually. It also keeps the team in a healthy cycle of self-evaluation.

Admonitions

The following admonitions address two critical temptations that most street workers will confront sooner or later: to quit and, due to heavy work loads, to become shoddy in the building of the ministry.

Never quit!

In the later years of his life, Winston Churchill made a visit to his childhood school. The appearance had been announced and everyone was expecting the statesman to make a speech. Enthusiasm was high; expectation was great. The moment finally came for Churchill to rise to the podium. His speech was short—unusually so: "Never . . . never . . . never . . . never give up!" Follow his advice.

Strive for excellency

"Approve what is excellent" (Philippians 1:10). Each Christian is a builder. We are to build our personal lives, our ministries and our families. Excellence must characterize our entire building process:

- ◆ Excellence is choosing the best available materials.
- ◆ Excellence is using our best available skills.
- ◆ Excellence is using faithfulness and integrity in the details of our lives and work (1 Corinthians 3:10-14).[6]

NOTES

1 Adapted from *Nehemiah: Builder of Walls, Leader of Men* by Glenn Johnson, (Manila: Action Publishing, 1993).

2 Leith Anderson, *Dying for Change* (Minneapolis: Bethany House, 1990), pp. 168-172.

3 Ibid., pp. 162-164.

4 Jerome Caluyio, Jr. and Henry R. Ruiz, *A Guide for Community Volunteers Working with Street Children* (Reach Up Project, Urban Basic Services Program in Olongapo City, Philippines).

5 Values clarification is helping the children integrate the cultural-traditional values that are accepted by their fellow citizens and not restricted to a region or language.

6 Lareau Lindquist, "Too Soon to Quit," in *Reflections on Encouragement*, Joe Musser, ed. (Rockford: Quadrus Media, 1994).

Appendix: Worksheet material for planning your ministry*

1. Defining your ministry
Is it to evangelize? Plant a church? Train leadership? Exercise social responsibility? A combination of these? Ultimately what do you want to see in the long term?

2. Understanding the street people in your target area
2.1 Basic data
What target group are you trying to reach (street children, sidewalk vendors, beggars, street families, prostitutes, etc.)?

What is the total number of your target group?

Describe your target group using the categories below:
Rate High (H) Medium (M), Low (L)

_____ Same language	_____ Common residential area
_____ Similar occupation	_____ Similar social class
_____ Racial/ethnic similarity	_____ Similar economic status
_____ Shared religious customs	_____ Shared hobby or interest
_____ Common kinship ties	_____ Discrimination from others
_____ Strong sense of unity	_____ Unique health situation
_____ Similar education level	_____ Similar age
_____ Common significant problems	_____ Other

2.2 Meaning system—worldview, thought processes and language
How well would street people say that you understand their worldview? The way they think? Their language?

Do you need to develop an understanding in any of these areas? Do you need assistance?

2.3 Needs
What are the felt needs of your target group? What opportunities for ministry do these needs open up?

2.4 Social structure
What has caused your target group to be on the streets?

*This material is adapted from *Crisis on the Streets: A Ministry Guide for Taking the Street Out of Street Children* (Third Edition), edited by Jeff Anderson and published by Action Publishing and Urban Street Ministries, Metro Manila, Philippines. Used by permission.

STREET CHILDREN

2.5 Receptivity of your target group to the gospel
Check the categories below that best describe your target group:

___ No awareness of Christianity	___ Aware Christianity exists
___ Some knowledge of the gospel	___ Understands gospel message
___ Recognize personal need of the gospel	___ Challenged to receive Christ
___ Have decided for Christ	___ Incorporated into the church
___ Active propagators of the gospel	

2.6 Christian witness/services offered
Investigate and list the various ministries/services offered among your target group.

Church/Mission/Agency	Year Begun	Number of Workers	Activities	Results

How are the ministries different?

Do they have resources that could help you in your ministry?

Do you have resources that could help them in their ministry or program?

3. The ministers
What type of person is needed to reach these people?

Qualities	Spiritual Gifts	Sensitivities	Personalities	Skills	Lifestyles
1. 2. 3. 4. 5. 6. 7. 8.					

Where can such people be found? What preparation and training do they need? What is your recruitment strategy?

Location for Recruits	Training/Preparation Needed	Recruitment Strategy
1. 2. 3. 4. 5. 6. 7.		

What are the implications for your own life? How must you change? What qualities and skills must you develop?

4. The methods
How do your methods relate to the receptivity of the people?

What methods are you currently using? How effective are they?

What kinds of new methods have been most effective in reaching, discipling or training these people?

What kinds of new methods could be tried?

5. Anticipated results
What obstacles do you anticipate in achieving your objectives?

What are possible solutions to overcoming these obstacles?

Think about this information. Pray over this information—individually and as a ministry group. What are the implications for your ministry? What are you doing right? What do you need to change?

13

Ready, set, engage! Gaining skills for counseling street youth

Mike DiPaolo

The Children

They sit on the sidewalk
Just look at those scared and lonely faces,
All of them hungry with toughened hearts.
Just sitting there day by day,
With nowhere to go
There's nowhere to play
Begging money from passers by,
Selling their bodies, jacking, or drugs,
Is there no other way to live?
These are runaways,
Fleeing from monsters at home.
Others are throwaways,
Not wanted anymore
Only to find more monsters and fears,
To find drugs and death
On the playgrounds of life!

—Christie

She was the kind of kid you look at and think to yourself, "My God, what a mess!" Nineteen going on forty, she had that haggard appearance that let you know what street life was like, and what it was costing her.

Yet for some reason that evening, she walked in our doors at Covenant House—the largest international agency serving homeless and runaway youth. (Covenant House provides food, shelter, medical care, counseling and other services for thousands of youth annually.) Why did she come in? Maybe she was in trouble, a pimp was after her or something like that, and she needed to hide out for a while.

Or maybe she had decided that enough is enough. She grew up in a home marred by physical and sexual abuse and alcoholism. Her parents were separated, and her own mother introduced her to the world of prostitution—a world from which she would take her identity at the tender age of eight years. The two "working women," mother and daughter, traveled around practicing their trade until mother was finally jailed for her exploits. This young girl also suffered the anxiety of being next to her father when he passed away from a disease related to his years of drinking.

With no history of a consistent home life, she fled for the bright lights of Hollywood—one of the world's major markets for runaways, attracting thousands each year. She would become one of those kids "left stranded, high and dry, on the concrete reefs of the city when shipwrecked families founder and go under."[1]

With no means of support, she turned to the one means of survival she knew—prostitution, commonly known as "survival sex"—because it is often the only option for survival for girls living on the streets. The abusive past from which she fled was now being reinforced by an abusive present, as the dangers of the street—physical beatings, rape and drug abuse just to name a few—befell her. "Is this what life is like? Am I really that worthless to be nothing more than an object for someone else's pleasure?" Such questions must have tormented her mind.

Yet she was resilient! How else could she survive this life, which had led her to the brink of death through multiple suicide attempts, and still be here tonight to walk into our doors? Yes, this resiliency had led Christie to decide that "enough was enough." She didn't know what this decision meant, nor the struggle it would entail. She didn't know what she wanted, only what she didn't want. But she made the choice. Now, it was our turn.

151

What can we do to help this desperate young woman? Just the thought of where to begin can be overwhelming. Add to that the realization that Christie's story is only one of literally millions of accounts about this virtually unknown population of "urban nomads," and we too can feel desperate. But there is hope. Like Christie, we must respond with resiliency in approaching this social dilemma. This chapter will explore some of the basics that can help us begin our work with street youth.

These kids have a problem: Our response to the public's attitude

Inevitably every time I talk with someone new about my work with street youth, I'm asked the same question, "What's wrong with these kids? Why are they out there?"

As counselors, it is always important to examine the popular culture's view of the population with whom we work. Historically, the notion of "runaway" has had many different meanings. During the first half of the twentieth century, public opinion was sympathetic to the needs of these youth. Perhaps the most popular runaway in American culture, Huck Finn, helped create an image of the fugitive as an "adventurer"—certainly a positive attribute.

But as the number of these "adventurers" started to grow, and with it their public visibility, a shift in attitude began. Their actions, such as those of hungry kids who need to take food from a market, were being examined in light of their economic and social impact. The "adventurers" were now seen as "problems." The professional response from the fields of psychology and social work would mirror this viewpoint. Early theories tabbed the runaway with deviant labels such as "psychoneurotic."[2] Such negative images culminated with the inclusion of "runaway reaction" as a psychiatric disorder in the second edition of the *Diagnostic and Statistical Manual*[3] (DSM-II), psychiatry's bible of mental disorders published in 1968.

Experts now believe Huck Finn had an innate mental problem. Certainly this would affect the attitudes of counselors working with these youth. *They* had a problem that needed to be fixed. As research with this population increased, however, our understanding of them began to change. *They* came from homes marred by physical and sexual abuse, drug and alcohol addiction and domestic violence. Their family and social histories made it increasingly clear that for the most part these were not "runaway" kids at all. They were "throwaways" or "pushouts," left with no other options but to turn to the street in the face of trauma. As such, their "problems," which are real, must be examined and treated in the light of a tremendously difficult childhood.

While this latter perception has emerged over the past twenty years or so, and social consciousness is beginning to be raised, it is important to note that, in general, public opinion has lagged far behind. The public attitude still more closely resembles the earlier viewpoint that "these kids are the problem." As counselors, we must expect to receive such reactions from the general public. Certainly this attitude maintains the invisibility of a population reaching upwards of two million in the United States alone.

Consider an example. The following is quoted from a brief article which appeared in *The Hollywood Reporter* in 1992:

> Brenda C., 22, was shot and killed in an alley behind Sunset Boulevard last Saturday night. Police say that the incident was gang and drug related. No suspects are known at this time.

Having known and worked with Brenda for a few years, I might offer the following slightly different version of this obituary:

> Brenda C., a 22-year-old single mother, was shot and killed in an alley behind Sunset Boulevard last Saturday evening. Brenda suffered from a disease which eventually forced her out of her family home. A lack of support for her children by their father further created an incredibly impoverished and difficult lifestyle for her. She is survived by her three children, ages 4, 2 and 1.

Is one of these articles more accurate? Certainly the newspaper's version of the story contains no lies. What it reported did happen. Yet my altered version illustrates that something is missing from the newspaper story. Its impersonal approach tends to maintain Brenda's anonymity and promotes the belief that she was just another bad kid who got what she deserved for being involved with drugs and gangs. By personalizing her, such a viewpoint becomes almost inhuman.

Thus part of our work as counselors of these youth is in the area of public education. To be the voices that help make them human in the eyes of society requires us to challenge ourselves as well. Taken at face value, the above newspaper article raises little speculation. But as we become more aware of the breadth of this issue, we must constantly look out for the things that promote the misperceptions or we, too, will become invisible to the children.

Recognition of these global effects is only half the battle. This negative public attitude has effects on the individual youth as well. All their lives they have been told how bad they are. Society at large now repeats what their parents first communicated to them. As the focus of this chapter moves toward our individual work with street youth, our understanding of not only where this attitude came from initially but also how it is being maintained will help us combat their often incredibly low self-perceptions.

Giving as a means of engaging: Our response to the individual street youth

After about two years of working with Christie, she turned to me and somewhat out of the blue stated, "I trust you, Mike. I'm not sure why, but I do."

Hanging on a wall immediately inside the front doors of every Covenant House program is its mission statement. Boldly standing out for all to see, perhaps the most moving part of this statement is its call to serve street youth with "absolute respect and unconditional love." These words provide a good starting point for our work, for it is the total acceptance of the individual as a person—not necessarily all that individual's actions—that provides the groundwork for our relationships and ultimately all our work with each street youth.

To begin to build a relationship we must display immediate respect for the individual. In some ways this may sound obvious, but never underestimate the power of basic human actions. This population has a very limited experience of healthy relationships with other human beings. Their value is in what they could provide for others, be it the punching bag for an abusive parent or the breadwinner for a pimp. Therefore, start simply and be genuine.

One premise of this approach asserts, "Give first before asking for anything in return." This giving may be something as simple as a name. Offer your name before asking for theirs. Street youth have had to give all their lives, usually without being asked, to the point where they almost literally have nothing but themselves. Certainly they have few physical possessions and little family support. Their names, however, are uniquely their own. Don't take that away too.

Another important way to display respect by giving first is to attempt to meet the immediate needs of these youth with no strings attached. Providing for their basic physical needs, such as food, clothing, or emergency medical attention, conveys a concern without an agenda. Typically, street youth have a very negative perception of any helping professional. Thus, if you approach them like a member of "the system," they will treat you as a part of it and you will fail to reach these kids, who are often called "system failures." The system would not give anything unconditionally, without asking at minimum for the completion of a large amount of paperwork.

As you engage street youth with absolute respect and unconditional love, they will begin to see that you are safe; you are providing a sanctuary for them and creating space in which change can occur. But don't push. The development of this initial trust is not an end point, it is only the beginning in a long process. It took two years for Christie to express her trust in me. What we may often take for granted in other relationships we cannot expect to find in our relationships with street youth. Remember who they are and where they come from. Remember that their trust has been violated routinely throughout their lives. They have had to learn to survive not by developing close relationships but by any means necessary.

Perhaps the most fundamental characteristic for a helper to practice in this process is listening. Regardless of your level of training or expertise—whether you are a psychologist, minister or lay person—listening to your client has an invaluable quality. To spend time genuinely listening to someone is at the core of building a relationship, and to do so with those who have not had these experiences in their lives can do wonders. Abusive parents do not listen, pimps do not listen, society does not listen—nobody listens, so listening distinguishes a concerned helper. By listening you validate the basic humanity and importance of the individual person, a direct contrast to the negative message that these are "bad kids."

What is listening? Listening is not giving advice or pity, nor is it a passive process. Rather, listening actively expresses a genuine desire to connect with the other person. If we could put listening into words, we would say, "This is your time. I am here for you . . . to hear who, and what, and where you are . . . to know you and possibly share part of me that you may use."

You must realize an important distinction: listening conveys empathy, not sympathy. Empathy is putting ourselves in the other person's shoes to gain a better understanding of who they are, not to feel sorry for them, but to put ourselves in a position to be of help.

In the initial stages we should let the street youth guide the discussion. Allow them to talk about themselves and their interests at their pace. Doing so further communicates respect and empowers them in the relationship. They will begin to feel a sense of control and see themselves as equals in the relationship, qualities necessary for effective work to be done. Street youth need your acceptance more than your wisdom. All the knowledge in the world won't help if a child feels worthless. Putting yourself in a position of authority, as the expert who has the answers to get them out of their predicament, only reinforces the message they have heard repeatedly—they are simply inferior.

So heed the credo, "When in doubt, listen." If you don't know what to say or don't have anything valuable to say (or sometimes even if you do), just listen. I feel that the incredible amounts of time spent listening to Christie's stories is what strengthened the bond in our relationship. At times it didn't feel like anything was being accomplished as she would go on and on, but in retrospect I know better. Listen, listen, listen!

Our overall goal as helpers in this engagement process is to be seen by the street youth as approachable, accepting and able to assist.[4] As you are getting to know the children, they are testing you, and you need to get three "A's" to pass this course. As alluded to earlier, these are children who often have been through the system only to end up on the streets. Others have tried to help, but their help was not effective. You now become their last hope before one of the only other remaining options—chronic homelessness, imprisonment or death—take over their young lives.

We can summarize the work of this engagement process under the title "value communication" (a term developed as one of the operating principles of Covenant House). Through our actions, more so than our words, our modus operandi is to treat others as we would want to be treated. Street life has its own code of values quite contrary to this one. This code is based on one principle—immediate gratification—and to obtain it requires that young people engage in many destructive behaviors that soon become normal to them. Through the value communication of giving respect and listening, we show them that there is another way, one based on trusting relationships and one that can lead them out of the self-destructive paths on which their lives are traveling.

Thank God they manipulate: A strengths-focused model of intervention

> *Christie would look at the ground, ashamed to even say the word "prostitution," which provided her means of survival. I said, "So you learned how to please other people because you had to in order to survive. Now let's see how you can use that ability in more healthy ways, including how to please yourself."*

Street youth manipulate. In fact, they are excellent at it. But let us take a closer look at that word "manipulate." It has been given such a negative connotation in today's language. Webster's Dictionary defines manipulate as "to manage or control artfully or by shrewd use of influence, especially in an unfair or fraudulent way."[5] That street youth are good at manipulation should be no surprise, for they have had to learn this active process to meet their own basic needs and survive. Looking at their histories enlightens our understanding of the development of these manipulative styles.

As infants and young children, these youth too often did not get the nurturing they needed at home. As a result, they had to develop alternate strategies to meet their needs. Basic psychological theories of personality posit that if children are not nurtured in those first years of life, they develop maladaptive ways of relating to other people and of gratifying their needs. The traumatic histories, the life stories of street youth, propel the development of these maladaptive patterns.

Once these children hit the streets, the patterns only intensify. The streets serve to reinforce these patterns, often hardening the child even more through the inevitable experiences of physical or sexual assault that await the child who flees to the street. Children become pawns in this cycle of violence simply because they need to survive. No one else has given to them, so they must learn to "manage and control their own lives artfully," i.e., manipulate. All too often, this need to survive entices the youth into petty theft or, worse yet, drug dealing and prostitution, two avenues initially seen as attractive for their financial rewards, but whose destructive impacts remain somewhat hidden. I have never known one child who came to Hollywood to be a drug dealer or a prostitute, but I certainly know many whose lives have become permanently scarred by being lured into these activities.

Now let's return to the present. Just because we as counselors or outreach workers come along with a smile (and maybe even engage the youth by giving respect and listening), should we expect street youth to readily accept our help and thereby break the pattern of manipulation? Of course not. Change does not happen overnight. Rather, we should expect them to manipulate us too. As discussed previously, these youth have no basis on which to trust us and for them to do so will be quite a lengthy process. We should expect manipulation such as lies about their age (to receive special services), or saying they didn't get anything to eat when they've already been given food. Their concern is for the immediate gratification of their hunger or need for shelter, or whatever will get them to the next day—not for building a relationship.

So how do we deal with this manipulation? Do we simply treat it as wrong, as punishable behavior (and therefore cast them off like everyone else in their life who has rejected them)? No. I say, "Thank God they manipulate." Only through this manipulation are they here with us today. Their manipulative actions served one purpose—survival; the survival of a small child in a turbulent house, the survival of a teen on a dangerous street. In fact, when street youth are not manipulating I begin to worry about such things as depression and suicidal thoughts setting in. Manipulation—an active process—tells me that the youth is still fighting for survival, fighting for a better life. When the fighting stops, the dying begins.

In the process of value communication, our goal becomes showing them another option. Just as they learned manipulation as an option, now it is time to be open to another. It is important not to chastise them for their manipulative styles. Instead help them recognize that manipulation is no longer necessary. Counting on the strength of your relationship, you can now take a more active and somewhat directive stance in challenging them to make changes in their lives.

In this process it is also important to remember the adage, "You can't take something away without replacing it with something else." Street youth already have so little that we cannot strip them of their means of survival (manipulation) without providing them with the tools to lead a more healthy lifestyle.

But once again, we know that change won't happen overnight. So when the inevitable act of manipulation recurs, be it big or small, our response can provide a turning point in our relationship with the youth. By expressing our willingness and desire to continue working with them despite this negative behavior, we communicate our acceptance of them as a person. In essence, we convey the simple message that they have worth, even when they do bad things.

What makes change so difficult for these youth? On the surface, it should seem that they would want to jump at the chance for a different life, and in many respects they do. But as humans we know that change fosters resistance. All too often it is easier to stay in the same situation, even if it is negative, than to make the change we know will be better for us. Street youth often view the pain of their current circumstance as less than the pain that change will require in terms of addressing some sensitive issues (e.g., abuse or drug dependency). Thus, they almost become comfortable with the pain. Perhaps a story will best illustrate this point.

A researcher named M. E. P. Seligman[6] designed an experiment in which he placed a dog inside a cage with an electrified grid at the bottom. He would administer a shock to the dog, causing it to make fruitless attempts at escape. Eventually realizing its predicament, the helpless animal would curl up and lie in a corner, simply accepting the painful shock. Then something fascinating happened. Seligman removed the top of the cage, so that the dog merely had to step over its low walls to escape. But when given further shocks, the huddled animal did not move. In fact, it took significantly more trials for the dog to learn to escape than to learn initially that it could not.

Seligman coined the term "learned helplessness" to describe this phenomenon, which we can apply to human behavior as well. After years of abuse—physical, sexual, emotional and verbal—street youth take on this learned helplessness. They come to expect that life is abusive and mistreatment will necessarily persist. Even when abuse is absent, they expect it will inevitably return. Like the dog who lay helplessly in the cage, they, too, feel no control over this process and, in effect, over their lives.

That is why it is so important for us to maintain that unconditional acceptance of these children as persons. That is why it is so important not to discourage the fight going on inside of them, even when its methods include manipulation. We need to repeatedly let them know that they are valued, for it is only when they come to believe it themselves that they will direct their energy on a more positive path.

As counselors, we cannot simply practice as technique the approach of maintaining a belief in the worth of these youth. If we do so, we are doomed to fail, for these incredibly perceptive youth will see right through us. We must accept as a core philosophical belief that these children possess many strengths, including the internal resources that can eventually enable them to make changes in their lives. One quality that always impresses me in my work with street youth is their resilience. I cannot begin to count how many times I've told Christie how resilient she is. These children are survivors. Their realities are worse than my nightmares, yet they possess the resiliency to keep going and keep the faith that things will get better.

With this belief system, our task as counselors is to plant the seeds of hope that can grow into change. For as much as I see their tremendous asset of resiliency, they are blind to it. They are like Seligman's dogs who do not realize that they have a way out. Too often, the most oppressive cages are those whose keys are locked in people's minds. It is our hope to guide the individual to find these keys.

This fundamental approach does not mean minimizing the emotional wounds that have resulted from the damaged histories of street youth. They have tremendous needs that must be addressed on the physical, psychological, social and spiritual levels. Typically, this requires extensive professional help, including that from multidimensional programs that can offer the necessary services. But never underestimate the impact one individual can have. It is often through the relationship to the one person who becomes the trusted other to the street youth that the greatest strides are made.

A hand up instead of a handout: Providing structure in chaotic lives

> *Christie confronting her reality: "Life for me has been a constant struggle—always running from my problems. . . . I'm afraid of what I might become as a person if I stay with the program, whatever that might be. I fear becoming real successful at what I do best, other than running away. I'm also afraid of losing, or not being able to succeed in this world."*

If the process of engagement provides the foundation of our work, then it is by providing structure that we build the walls of this house. The approach of the proposed belief system does not discount the negative behaviors of street youth that must be addressed. The positive qualities discussed, such as resilience, are attributed to the individual person—a great need, given their histories. Nevertheless, we cannot overlook the negative behaviors if we are to hope for change.

We must provide for these youth by putting order back into their chaotic lives. A turbulent home and spontaneous street life do not foster the development of an organized lifestyle. At home, the children must act out to get attention, for even negative attention from a parent is better than no attention. We must expect that they will test us with similar behaviors, because they have an unconscious belief that they must act out to gain our attention too. An initial way of communicating structure then becomes consistent in our response. We accept the person but place limits on what are acceptable behaviors. Being consistent in our setting limits is extremely important if we are to be seen as strong in the eyes of the street youth. If they see us wavering, we risk losing their respect.

The streets are the antithesis of structure. There, acting out often takes the form of impulsive and self-destructive behaviors. Life is lived moment to moment, day to day, with no sense of being oriented toward the future. We must attempt to show them that there is a future worth striving for, and by setting the groundwork now they can build for that future. What this requires is some sense of organization, self-discipline or what I'm calling structure. Many youth, such as Christie, are at the point where they realize that street life is a dead end when they choose to let a counselor or outreach worker intervene. Christie made the decision to get off the street but really didn't know what she wanted. She was at this point where day-to-day existence was taking the breath of her very life. She knew it could not continue but needed us to begin showing her another way.

The type of structure we provide is different from more traditional notions. In many respects, it is a formalized system of rules and regulations against which street kids are revolting that has led them to the streets. Their flight to the streets is a flight from the control of this imposing structure. When we implement some sense of structure, we cannot be perceived as trying to regulate their lives. While there must be clear parameters of the structure (in terms of acceptable behavior), there must be room within it to allow for growth. This strategy creates choices for the individual youth, empowering them with a sense of control over the direction of the relationship and of the change each individual desires to make.

Structure serves a function similar to a map, filling in the gaps of how to move from start to finish on a journey. The "maps" we create with street youth involve developing an individualized plan of their goals and objectives. Structure provides the tools to successfully negotiate this journey, teaching fundamental processes such as decision making and problem solving. Furthermore, embedded in this structure are the values of a more healthy lifestyle that we hope will become embedded in the youth as they move away from the street lifestyle.

Structure also serves a function similar to that of a container, in this case a container for their emotions. In this metaphor, street youth have typically developed without a great sense of internal control. Their emotions spill over in the form of inappropriate, acting out behavior. Again this should not surprise us given their histories in which their helplessness was fostered by the people who controlled them. By placing limits on what are acceptable behaviors, we encourage street youth to express their emotions within the space of this container, or of this structure. We hope that having defined boundaries will translate into their learning how to express themselves appropriately without going too far, or spilling over. In essence, this structure helps street youth learn how to develop more healthy interpersonal relationships.

Introduce structure at different levels based on the level of relationship with the youth. In the beginning, when our primary goal is to engage the youth, we may not require much structure. Structure is primarily communicated by our unconditional acceptance of the youth and our consistency in working with them.

Only as the relationship develops can we increasingly challenge the negative behaviors and destructive lifestyle more directly. This may reach a point of placing conditions on their receiving some or all of the services we provide. For example, we may not offer to find shelter for drug abusing youth who are unwilling to face their addiction. Ultimately, we want to communicate that we are there and will be there for the individual, but we cannot tolerate negative behavior. If we do so correctly, then this does not come across as rejection. Our goal is not to communicate that the youth is worthless, but that they are worth more than the behaviors that now control them.

In many respects, structure communicates to the street youth that we are serious about giving them a hand up, not just a hand out. We want them to turn their lives around, but are aware of the struggle this will entail and respect their choices in undertaking or not undertaking this process.

While this implies a very serious choice, note that the essence of structure is human. It is not that formalized system of rules and regulations that will turn off the street youth because they have failed at it before. Rather, structure must have a degree of flexibility so it can adapt to the needs of the individual. If we ask too much of youth who are not ready to change, we set them up for failure. If we do not ask enough, then we are colluding to maintain their current predicament. Street youth are at different points, and we are at different points in our relationship with them; this means using a level of structure that is appropriate to each individual. In each case our goal is to provide a structure which both promotes and challenges growth, while empowering the youth to make those choices required to achieve growth.

Helping you or helping me? Maintaining professionalism in our work

> Christie had made the decision to return home where a new step-father (her mother was still in jail) wanted to provide for her. She didn't want to talk about it. She could probably sense my disapproval of the idea, and in some ways probably knew of its futility herself. But the desire to recapture the absent family is so strong. Nevertheless, I respected her choice to go. However, not until four months later (when the situation ended in another suicide attempt and she finally called me) did Christie realize my position, having assumed that I rejected her because of her decision. She came back to Covenant House to try again. And we welcomed her.

Just as we set limits and boundaries for the youth we serve, as counselors we must establish professional limits and boundaries in our relationships with them. The needs of street youth can be very draining on us, and we can find ourselves trying to make up for the years of neglect they have suffered. This urge propels a strong desire within us to do more, to extend ourselves unknowingly beyond our capabilities. We must realize that we, as individual counselors, can never fully provide what these youth need. When we attempt to do so, the relationship becomes over-personalized, causing us to lose sight of our professional goals and inevitably to fail in our work. We become another in the long string of individuals who have made broken promises and not come through for the youth.

Along these same lines, it is vital to remember this: Never make a promise that you can't keep. Often the most well-intentioned acts turn into our biggest failures, for not only do they damage the relationship but, even worse, they push the youth further into the destructive lifestyle of the street.

Thus, it is important that we evaluate ourselves as counselors. Discussing our personal reactions with colleagues, supervisors or even those to whom we turn for counsel is a must. This accountability will help us maintain a more team-oriented and ultimately a more professional approach.

Perhaps most important in this process is our own self-evaluation. We all want to help, to do good, but often this, too, is a struggle, requiring us to challenge our own feelings of insecurity and inadequacy. Sometimes we may overcompensate by trying to be a "savior," a process that really does more to meet our own needs than those of the youth we serve. As alluded to earlier, our approach to working with this challenging population of street youth cannot simply be one of technique—we must invest ourselves in it. But to be effective, this personal investment requires us to maintain professional boundaries.

The following is a list of common counselor reactions in their relationships with clients. It can be used as an internal checks and balances system in the ongoing process of self-evaluation:

Am I getting too personal?
- Do I have a desire to "rescue" the youth or fix his or her situation or feelings to make myself feel competent, less worried about the youth, powerful, or less "helpless?"

- ◆ Do I have feelings of being morally, intellectually, behaviorally, emotionally or otherwise superior to the youth?
- ◆ Do I have the desire to "prove" to the youth that my view is "right" (with an emphasis on proving its rightness versus helping them)?
- ◆ Do I have feelings of frustration or impatience with the youth's behavior, lack of progress or resistance to being helped (e.g., when he or she puts up walls toward me)?
- ◆ Do I take a youth's negative response as an attack and feel a need to get defensive about it (e.g., his or her being critical of me, asserting "superiority" or being angry at me)?
- ◆ Do I fear that the youth is evaluating me and will become angry with me, disapprove of me or see me as incompetent?
- ◆ Do I fail to consider whether any of a youth's negative feedback to me might be true or useful in my own self-examination?

Certainly it is not wrong to have any or all of these reactions; they are quite normal. As counselors we should be concerned if we are not aware of having any of them. It may mean that we are not investing ourselves fully into our work, or that we don't know ourselves very well.

The important part of this self-examination is what we do with these reactions. We need to talk about the thoughts and feelings that arise in our work with street youth. This work can often bring out our most sensitive vulnerability, whether through the intentional act of a youth "pushing our buttons" for some manipulative purpose, or through some seemingly innocuous act which unintentionally triggers a response inside us.

Our intention as counselors is to find a healthy balance in our work, one which enables us to invest fully in our work without burning out. This balance will further enable us to develop healthy relationships with the youth. The analogy of cradling an injured bird in one's hand can be applied here. If we hold it too loosely, it will flap away and die. If we hold it too tightly, it will suffocate and die. Only by finding the healthy balance can we nurture it back to health, and thereby develop the bond that will foster its coming back to us even when we release it.

Analogously we cannot be too loose in our work with street youth; they need structure. Nor can we impose our own agenda too strongly; we need to respect their right of choice. Attempting to achieve the balance is more difficult than taking either of the extremes. But this is the only way we can be nurturing, for we know that they will inevitably leave our nests often needing someday to return.

To sum up this need to maintain a professional balance in our work, I might offer the following (yet another!) adage: "Love them with your heart, but think with your head."

Ready, set, engage! Some concluding remarks on working with street youth

Some three years after that resilient girl first walked in the doors of Covenant House, there was a change in Christie's tone of voice, and in the words too: "I feel better about myself. I want to do good things for me now. That sounds different, doesn't it?"

As I began work on this project, Christie was residing in a state psychiatric hospital, a place she inhabited a few times before when the streets were winning the battle. Now, months later, she is out and doing better for herself. She still comes by Covenant House but not because she is in crisis. Rather she wants to maintain the connection she has developed with me and a few others who have known her over these past years and to get some support as she continues her upward struggle.

Will she be in crisis again? Will she achieve independence? These things I can't be certain about but I do know that she now believes in herself enough to work toward taking some positive steps in her life.

On the surface it may seem funny that her assertion provides the conclusion for this chapter, as it seems more like a starting than an ending point. That someone should "want to do good things" for themselves is taken for granted. But such assumptions overlook the despair that is the reality of being on the streets. We cannot define "success" in working with street youth by the things that they achieve but in the individual growth as represented in Christie's words.

When Christie first came to us, the streets were killing her. Then she only knew what she didn't want. Now, years later, she may actually be at the point to believe in herself enough to know what she does want. And to hear her make this one proclamation is all that a humble counselor could ever hope for.

NOTES

1   B. Ritter, *Covenant House: Lifeline to the Street* (New York: Random House, 1987).

2   N. Stefanidis, "Attachment Antecedents of Runaway Youth: A Profile of a Treatment Responsive Runaway," unpublished doctoral dissertation, California School of Professional Psychology, Los Angeles, 1988.

3   *American Psychiatric Association, Diagnostic and Statistical Manual of Mental Disorders*, 2nd edition (Washington, D.C.: American Psychiatric Press, 1968).

4   P. Morrissette, "Engagement strategies with reluctant homeless young people" in *Psychotherapy* (1992:29, pp. 447-451).

5   *Webster's New Twentieth Century Dictionary*, 2nd edition (New York: Simon and Schuster, 1983).

6   M.E.P. Seligman, S.F. Maler and J. Geer, "The alleviation of learned helplessness in the dog," in *Journal of Abnormal Psychology* (1968:78, pp. 256-262).

PART FIVE:

Alternatives to Life on the Street

14

Principles for effective intervention planning

Phyllis Kilbourn

Building a strong foundation is important whether you are referring to a physical structure, a developing child's life or an effective rehabilitation program for street children. The following basic principles, though by no means inclusive, will enable workers to lay a strong foundation upon which to build their programs.

Prevention: A foundational principle

Early detection and prevention of problems is an undergirding principle and initial building block in all outreaches to street children. As the age-old adage claims, "An ounce of prevention is worth a pound of cure."

Families

Finding solutions to family problems can prevent children from being forced onto the streets. Prevention will include identifying vulnerable children and their families; helping families identify the source of their problems; enabling families to cope with their living situations by helping them acquire the necessary skills to earn a living; providing assistance for the

171

children to attend school; and strengthening disintegrating family life.

Carolyn Brown and Susan Little[1] emphasize that when working with families that "are at risk," it is important to treat each family as unique and important. Obviously an approach that values the strength and uniqueness of each family and offers a relationship of support and encouragement will make an impact on the lives of the families, the children and the entire community.

Brown and Little's model of intervening with families holds the common thread of "reframing," understood as helping the parents and child see problems in a new way to invite creative solutions.

The Nurture Program, described by Fran Kaplan, has had a successful history of preventing and treating child abuse. The model has been adapted for use across ethnic groups and socio-economic levels. Kaplan outlines four parental behaviors that the Nurture Program targets for change:

> 1) Excessive demands on children's performance or unreasonable expectations of what they [are] capable of—emotionally, socially, physically and intellectually;
>
> 2) A lack of awareness, understanding and respect for the needs and feelings of children as people;
>
> 3) Reliance on the use of physical force and pain (spanking, whipping, locking children out of the house and such), or on using hurtful and humiliating words to control children's behavior; and
>
> 4) Adults' dependence on their children for physical and emotional comfort, companionship, and validation of their own worth.[2]

As a response to these behaviors, the Nurture Program uses a variety of psycho-educational techniques (such as role-playing, games, music, discussion and infant massage) to encourage growth in the following areas: appropriate expectations, empathy, non-violent behavior management/conflict resolution and proper family hierarchy. The program staff encourage parents to try new behaviors, yet offer support as these families step into unfamiliar territory.

172

Jill Kinney, Kelly Dittmar and Wendy Firth have outlined the Homebuilders Model for working with families in crisis. The foundation to their interventions is the conviction that "it is best for families to learn how to handle their own problems."[3] The "homebuilders" caseworkers join with the families as colleagues and coach them in the home. The caseworkers are "on-call" for the families twenty-four hours a day and the commitment to the families is an intensive four to eight weeks. Each caseworker coaches two families at a time (otherwise the on-call status could be overwhelming).

The families learn and practice necessary skills in limit setting, emotional control and setting effective rewards and punishments. Kinney, Dittmar and Firth report that families appreciate the in-home services provided. Not only is it convenient for them, but the homebuilder counselor feels like a friend coming to help.

A home-based model, such as the Homebuilder Model, may work in an urban or rural neighborhood setting. A community may already have certain older members that have the informal role of "parenting expert." The "community grandmothers" can offer guidance and encouragement, or they may simply help in daily tasks such as cooking or cleaning. Identifying these natural community resource people and using their wisdom can add a sense of community responsibility and commitment to the issue of prevention. The community members themselves can determine how this support can be offered to families in a culturally appropriate way, in order to avoid at-risk families feeling stigmatized.

John P. Ronnau offers four basic principles that may act as a framework to guide programs for prevention of family breakdown:[4]

> *Principle 1:* An active role by family caregivers is critical in enabling their child to live in a normal environment;
>
> *Principle 2:* Family caregivers themselves can best articulate their own needs and those of their children;
>
> *Principle 3:* Services should be provided in caregiver's homes or in other settings where they are most comfortable; and

173

Principle 4: The relationship between caregivers and service providers is the key to making the helping process work.

All strategies must include principles that help families improve or change their circumstances. If the family cannot be held together, the potential street child should have viable options available to him or her before being forced into street life.

Paul Jones[5] recognizes the children that have been orphaned or separated from their caregivers. Prevention may seem an impossible issue for these children. The community itself, however, may offer a haven of support that can keep children without parents or guardians away from life on the street.

Advocacy

Another important element in prevention is engaging in advocacy on behalf of children and their families. Governments often provide for the rights of children to assistance such as proper care and nutrition and special protection from neglect, abuse and exploitation. Many nations have signed the UN's Convention on the Rights of the Child or other similar national child's rights agreements. Advocating on behalf of the children's rights can be a powerful tool in prevention strategies.

Basic principles: An holistic approach

Street children are faced with many challenges and pressures arising from such problems as lack of access to education and employment, difficulties arising from family problems or lack of community support. They encounter poverty, undernourishment, hunger, unsanitary and unhealthy living conditions, drugs, susceptibility to diseases, injuries and accidents from street life or physical and sexual abuse by older children and adults.

The children also are deprived of parental support, discipline, basic social services and guidance. They often develop serious problems related to emotional deprivation. Clearly these children need interventions that incorporate strategies to meet their economic, social, physical, emotional, educational, training, spiritual and moral needs.

174

Keep projects simple and indigenous

Due to the immensity of the problem and the lack of extensive resources, keep models of intervention simple and indigenous in nature. Annette Cockburn states, "In these contexts, the 'less for more' principle must inform our practice."[6]

You do not need vast amounts of money or large, specially built premises to start a local program. Research existing local resources such as churches or community centers, and involve families and community leaders as volunteer help. Some local organizations may be willing to provide resources such as the business community, the national Red Cross or church agencies.

Plan community-based programs

Along with sensitivity to the local culture, you also must be sensitive to the value of a community-based program. Community leaders will have insights that will prove invaluable to understanding the children's problems and to assist in planning the programs to meet the children's needs. Once a community embraces ownership of a project, the project is much more likely to succeed. Developing community mobilization and community councils also can be an asset in preventing the breaking of laws or causing legal problems because of ignorance.

Understand your primary resource

Remember that the primary resource in any program or strategy is the children themselves. It is imperative that workers get to know and understand the children before attempting programs or projects to assist them. The children are the experts; they know what their deepest concerns, problems and needs are as well as their aspirations for the future. Unless you listen to and address their concerns in your intervention planning, they will not be eager to listen to what you have to teach or provide.

Once you gain an understanding of the children and their needs, it can be helpful to use the children as educators and public relations (PR) channels. This is especially successful when you can identify the group or gang leaders the children have chosen. These leaders are most apt to have earned the children's confidence and respect.

Beware of creating special groups and dependency

Most projects start with the idea of providing food or shelter. Unless the children are hungry, there may be no need to provide food. They also may have no need for special buildings. We must be cautious in presenting ourselves as able to supply all their needs and wants. Nothing is free in life and the children know it. We must not put them in a world of our dreams.

You must also be cautious about separating girls from boys, for example, when it comes to offering project services. Many projects tend to favor girls, creating a feeling of dependency. If you make differences between groups of children, you must have valid reasons for doing so. Discuss these reasons with the children.

Also be on guard not to break up "gang families" when setting age limits. Stan Guthrie describes how this happened in a new street children's project in Medellin, Colombia. "When we started this thing, we said we were only going up to age 12. But we quickly found out that to get to the entire pack, you have to allow the older boys to come because they are the leaders of the pack."[7]

Remove obstacles

A major stumbling block to successful programs can be our own attitudes. Workers must be willing to look beyond the dirt, the rebellion and their revulsion of the children's lifestyle, to loving and valuing the children as Jesus did. Workers cannot expect children to change their lifestyles if they have no sense of their own self-worth. Children will not gain this idea of valuing themselves unless you consistently express respect for them. Remember not to see street children as passive recipients of care. They are survivors in their own right and you must respect them as such. Children also must learn that in God's eyes they are precious and of utmost worth.

Use a multilevel approach

There is no one strategy that will work for every street child, so you will need many approaches as the children move through the phases of rehabilitation. There should be an increase of basic services to address the needs of these children both on and off the street. The Homestead in South Africa, presented in the next chapter, is an outstanding example of a multilevel program.

Provide alternatives

Often children cannot resist the lure of street life. If they are to leave the streets, you must give them a challenging alternative to street life. Along with the hardship and dangers associated with street life, the children enjoy many benefits. They become bonded to their friends, a bonding that can become as strong as that of children to their parents. They deeply identify with one another and have learned to pull together to survive. They also come to feel secure and to enjoy the sense of belonging they experience within the relationships they have formed.

Examine your motivation

It is vital for all workers to examine their motivation for working with street children. Avoid allowing the vulnerability of these children to satisfy the emotional needs of the adults concerned. We must go beyond feelings of mere pity to a genuine compassion that enables us to identify with the children's feelings and needs.

Investigate networking

Networking is vital to conserve limited time and resources. It is worth taking a little extra time to research resources of the community, church, non-governmental organizations (NGOs) or existing projects before launching a new program. A network that can provide such information may already be in place; if not, it could prove valuable to form one for mutual sharing of resources and experiences, to avoid duplication of efforts and to provide feedback and evaluation.

Plan for reintegration

Returning the children to their families must always be an ultimate goal for consideration. Frequently street educators are the first point of contact with families and can serve as the catalyst for change, which sometimes results in the reintegration of children into their families.

For successful reintegration to occur, the root causes that drove the child from the home must be addressed and removed. This usually includes exploring ways to improve the economic life of the family. Where there has been child abuse, the parents and child must receive counseling. While reconciliation and healing is to be sought at all costs, often it is not possible to achieve. Sometimes the children are too emotionally scarred by being beaten, left hungry or neglected too much.

Voluntary participation

For the child who has taken to life on the streets, independence is a most valued possession. Despite the disadvantages and dangers of living on the streets, children enjoy being free to come and go as they please, not being controlled by any adult and having a measure of control over their lives. Attempts to place them in a safe, secure environment usually results in their taking what they want from adults they have little genuine respect for and whose motives they may not trust. Frequently the children respond by running away again.

Thus any real project for street children has to address their tendency to run away from problems that occur instead of discussing and solving them. For these reasons, voluntary participation in the program is another important element in successful programs. The children must be allowed to feel that they are taking charge of changing their circumstances—not being coerced to do so. Because they often reject authority figures as hypocritical and punitive, voluntary attendance is an essential attractor.[8]

Vital principles of Covenant House

Central to the development of the Covenant House program model for a youth care facility are five vital principles of operation: immediacy, sanctuary, values communication, structure and choice.[9] These principles provide a framework for all the principles utilized in structuring programs to target street children and, as such, provide a suitable conclusion to this chapter.

Immediacy highlights the importance of locating the children's centers within the immediate area of their needs. For children on the run, the difference between a short walk and waiting for the correct subway train is often the difference between whether or not they get help. Immediacy also requires that the center is open 24 hours a day, seven days a week; that counselors practice immediacy through an "open intake," that is, no youth is turned away at his or her first time at the center; and that the children are accepted and offered immediate services through a specially trained intake team.

Sanctuary, or safety, has to do with the entire environment of care that the young person experiences. By definition, sanctuary is a refuge or place of safety. Counselors are selected and trained to ensure that each young person is protected from the dangers of the streets. Youngsters also are protected from harsh judgments concerning their pasts. Sanctuary also includes seeing that the center is a clean and comfortable environment for the children. Such an environment helps to reestablish in each child a sense of dignity and self-worth, necessary early steps to further counseling.

Values communication demands that children in the center tell the truth, care about themselves, respect others and start working on plans of activity with counselors and social workers. Youth in the intake and diagnostic sessions are told that such rules as "no drugs or alcohol, no use of violence (verbal or physical), and 'be human'" are all parts of a value system that is different from the value system of the street.

Structures in a residential program are the parameters of the individual and group relationships, as well as the rituals and accountability systems for the rules and procedures in the center. In time each youth, together with the therapeutic team, is responsible for working out a realistic, short-term plan for himself or herself—a return home or to school or to start preparing for a job and eventual independent living.

Choice includes the awareness and knowledge of options, and the selection of alternatives that will bring about growth and development. Within the principle of choice is the encouragement, and at times the confrontation, by the counseling staff in order to help the young people break their destructive choices for "the street" and to support their choices toward "the good."

Dividends

Taking the extra time required to lay a solid foundation for your programs will pay rich dividends. Your efforts will result in effective programs that not only are acceptable to the children, but also are beneficial to their healing and to the restoration of hope in their young lives.

NOTES

1   Carolyn L. Brown and Susan Little, "Family Reunification," in *Children Today* (Nov./Dec. 1990), p. 21.

2   "Nurturing Skills Training for Parents and Children: Antidote to Abuse," a paper presented at the Tenth International Congress on Child Abuse and Neglect in Kuala Lumpur, Malaysia, September 13, 1994. (Family Development Resources, Inc., 3160 Pinebrook Road, Park City, Utah, 84060 U.S.A.).

3   Jill Kinney, Kelly Dittmar and Wendy Firth, "Keeping Families Together," in *Children Today* (Nov./Dec. 1990), pp. 14-19.

4   John P. Ronnau, "A Strengths Approach to Helping Family Caregivers," in *Children Today* (Nov./Dec. 1990), pp. 24-27.

5   Paul Jones, "Ministering to Street Children," in *Together* (No. 32, 1991), pp. 3-5.

6   Annette Cockburn, "Looking After Street Children: A Model Indigenous to South Africa," a paper presented at the Tenth International Congress on Child Abuse and Neglect in Kuala Lumpur, Malaysia, September 10-13, 1994.

7   Stan Guthrie, "Ministry to Medellin Street Kids Offers Hopeless a Second Chance," in *Pulse* (March 6, 1992), p. 3.

8   David Vincent, "The Street Children of Quelimane, Mozambique, Part II," in *City Watch* (Vol. 10, No. 3), p. 2.

9   Herbert J. Freudenberger and Stephen E. Torkelson, "Beyond the Interpersonal: A System Model of Therapeutic Care for Homeless Youth and Children," in *Psychotherapy* (Vol. 21, No. 1, Spring 1984).

15

Effective intervention strategies: A compilation

Phyllis Kilbourn

Multilevel approaches

This chapter includes examples of the many successful intervention programs launched to assist street children. These models will enable you to witness "in action" some vital intervention principles presented in the last chapter. These examples also should spark ideas for your own intervention planning.

The Homestead of Cape Town, South Africa, was chosen as a basic intervention model that incorporates a multilevel approach. This comprehensive program evolved from the children's changing needs as they progressed through the various phases of rehabilitation. The Homestead is widely accepted in South Africa as a model for intervention in the care, education and reintegration of children into their families.

UFM International presents a comprehensive action plan in outline form. You can adapt their model successfully to meet specific program needs.

The Homestead's director, Annette Cockburn,[1] shares the

181

philosophy and structure of the Homestead project in the following section.

The Homestead's philosophy

The Homestead has a simple mission: "To help street children reconstruct their shattered lives." The model for accomplishing this mission is not only indigenous, but also effective and affordable. The model is based on a developmental imperative: interventions should be multifaceted to address the needs of the children as they move through the phases of rehabilitation.

The following four key features, which are vital to any program for street children, characterize the philosophy of this model.

Organic growth

When the Intake Centre became too full of settled children, a second stage children's home, The Bridge, was opened to cater to the more stable population. When it was discovered that returning children to formal school too soon was counterproductive and largely unsuccessful, the nonformal education program known as "Learn and Live" was started. The structures are from bottom up rather than top down.

Simplicity

The Homestead offers very simple services in a phased rehabilitation program geared to meet the children's needs at different developmental stages. The Homestead does not have an elaborate infrastructure of employees such as clerks, drivers, cooks or fund raisers. The staff consists of child care workers with some input from social workers and educators. A commitment has been made to offer basic services to the maximum number of children both on and off the street; the "less for more" principle informs the Homestead's practices.

Transparency

The center's policies, protocols, finances and facilities are always open to scrutiny. Visits, comments and debate are encouraged. The children are self-referred to the program and an "open door" policy is maintained.

Accountability

The organization maintains a policy of scrupulous accountability to funders, state departments, the public and to the children themselves.

The Homestead model

The first contact the children have with the Homestead is usually through the street workers. The role of the street worker is multifaceted. Tasks include monitoring the health and nutritional status of the children still living on the streets and fulfilling an advocacy role with the police and juvenile justice system.

The street worker is a relatively cheap resource having the potential of reaching hundreds of children and, due to prompt attention to children newly on the streets, can initiate preventive measures and refer the most vulnerable to appropriate resources.

Yizani Drop-in Centre

Yizani means "come everybody" in Xhosa. The program evolved from the needs of the children as expressed to street workers: "Where can we find you when we need you? Where can we sleep safely and wash?"

Yizani offers children still living on the street basic recreational and educational activities along with access to food, medical care and showers. Yizani encourages street children to make choices. Since its inception, the biggest change has been observed in the behavior of the children. Initially children would abuse solvents, refuse to allow other groups into the center, behave atrociously, steal, fight and carry on as though there were no tomorrow. Now children do not bring their drugs into the center and only occasionally does a child enter the center "high." There are few fights and only in extreme circumstances will a child resort to violence to vent frustration. Racism and intimidation among the children are no longer endemic.

Educational and recreational activities include language development, AIDS education, street law, art, clay work, drama, wire work, music, soccer and swimming. The children are involved in a tin can recycling project.

Yizani has only a few, but nonnegotiable, rules: No solvents or knives, nobody over 16 years of age and a five block exclusion zone—you are either in the center, or five blocks away. There is to be no loitering outside, fighting, sniffing glue, irritating the neighbors or attracting such undesirable elements as drug dealers to the area.

Between three to five hardened street children leave Yizani every month to admit themselves to more formal programs and shelters. Some children return home, some find informal jobs, most improve their lives in one way or another. Yizani does not pretend to be a total solution. The center is only open four hours a day, five days a week, catering to those children initially unable or unwilling to refer themselves to a shelter or to return home.

The Bridge: A night shelter

The Homestead identified a gap in services for children and youth for whom even the minimal structures of the Intake Centre (see below) were too difficult, or who were not eligible for admission (those over sixteen). For these, The Bridge was opened to provide a link between the street and more formal resources.

The Bridge is open only at night. There is a dormitory for very young children, girls or children with AIDS. In keeping with the Homestead's ethos of functional services to a maximum number of children, the Bridge, like the other projects, does not have managers or coordinators, nor is it a custodial bureaucracy. The program does not offer therapy or even full-time residential care. It simply offers some hope along with a safe, dry, warm place to sleep; soup and bread at night; and porridge in the morning. The building design allows the children to use the outside bathroom facilities during the day.

The Intake Centre

The Intake Centre is quite literally a door onto the street and, in this, is extraordinarily appropriate. The transition from pavement to shelter can be immediate and nonthreatening. Many children come to the Intake Centre after visiting the Yizani Drop-in Centre or sleeping at the Bridge night shelter.

The Centre is usually overcrowded, noisy, often tense, but never dull. The children are generally wild and unsocialized,

184

considered by local welfare agencies to be among the most damaged and deprived in the area. They are also lively, engaging, outgoing, often compassionate and in some ways hauntingly perceptive.

The Intake Centre's criteria and admission procedures are simple. Children between age six and sixteen living on the streets must come to the Centre of their own free will. Once there they are given a shower, clean clothes and a meal; then they are given time to adjust. If the children settle in, they are screened at the venereal disease, tuberculosis and dental clinics. A social worker sees them and the process of rehabilitation continues.

Learn to Live: A nonformal education program

At this stage a child may have been in contact with a street worker, attended Yizani Drop-in Centre, slept at the night shelter and then admitted himself or herself to the Homestead Intake Centre where the rehabilitation continues. Inherent in this process is the societal assumption that the child will be returned to school. This raises a number of questions.

The Cape Town Child Welfare Society has produced convincing data to support the hypothesis that children in alternate care "fail to thrive" in existing school structures. This fact is illustrated most dramatically in the case of the street child whose problems at school figure prominently in his or her reason for being on the street in the first place.

Yet, a central tenet in the process of rehabilitation is that children return to the very institution which has painful and alienating associations for them. The Homestead determined that there was a need for an educational alternative, a need which became a powerful imperative.

In an attempt to address this need, the Homestead embarked on a program called "Learn to Live." The project is based on an adult education model of nonformal education. With street children, we are looking at a group that confounds the concept of "child." In many ways the children live on the streets as functional adults and need educational strategies that recognize this.

Learn to Live's main aims are:

1) To accustom the child to a structured day. The lives of children on the street lack almost any form of structure. Yet,

readjustment to structure is crucial if re-entry to formal schooling is to be successfully accomplished.

2) To equip the child, who may never have been at school or who has been on the street for some time, with the necessary remedial skills required for admission to the formal school system.

3) To provide vocational training for those youngsters who, by virtue of their age or aptitude, are not school material. They are apprenticed to either a printing press or to a metal workshop.

Learn to Live employs enough teachers so the groups of children can be kept small, enabling the teachers to provide more individual attention. The children are taught in their mother tongue.

Patrick's House: A home for boys

Once a boy has been through some of the stages of rehabilitation, has settled at the Intake Centre, sleeps there every night and attends the non-formal education project regularly, he will be considered for admission to Patrick's House—the final phase of the program. This is a registered home for boys where all the boys attend formal school in the community or are at Learn to Live.

It is at Patrick's House that the Homestead's successes are most visible. The boys there are largely indistinguishable from teenagers anywhere. The blare of pop music is endemic, an avid interest is taken in clothes, they belong to soccer clubs, enter competitions and so on. Many return to host families and their own parents for weekends and holidays. A few have full-time jobs and are being eased out of the nest.

Homestead's next project will have to be an independent living program. Perhaps it will take the form of a couple of communal houses where working boys, with minimal supervision, will learn to budget, shop, practice life skills and become autonomous, empowered members of the communities in which they will live their adult lives.

UFM International: Brazil

UFM International, with over sixty years of experience in Brazil, is now expanding into an holistic ministry to street children. Their action plan incorporates three phases and serves as an excellent guideline for those organizing a program for street children.

1) Contact stage
   ◆ Outreach in plazas, slums, on bridges and streets
   ◆ Establish "contact centers" in key locations (provide meals, medical care and "TLC"—tender loving care)
   ◆ Develop camping programs
2) Reconciliation and rehabilitation stage
   ◆ "Connect" with a "spiritual family"
   ◆ Reconnect with family (if there is one)
   ◆ Training centers (literacy, trade skills)
   ◆ Discipleship and resocialization
   ◆ Judicial care and adoption
3) Reintegration and normalization
   ◆ Solid integration into a family and church
   ◆ Expanded professional training

Long-term rehabilitation programs

Providing hope for the children's future gives them an incentive to change their lifestyle and to apply diligent effort to bring about meaningful change in their lives. Vocational programs have been successful in accomplishing these objectives.

Cooperatives

Thomas Teage, executive director of the Child Assistance Program (CAP) in Liberia, sought to help children who were forced to make the streets their home due to the civil war. His theory of cooperatives as a framework for training and employment stemmed from the children's experiences and knowledge obtained through their war-related experiences as street children and combatants. The children had learned to live in gangs and to pull together for survival.

The goal of CAP is to provide a yearlong training program that includes literacy training, cooperative skills, animal husbandry (pigs, rabbits and poultry) and agricultural skills.

After one year of training the children will form cooperatives. They may choose to specialize in agriculture or animal husbandry. CAP hopes to provide each child with a plot of land or an animal to get them started in the business of their choice. To launch their cooperatives, the children will also be offered a loan to start their business. The children will govern themselves, making their own rules and decisions—how to spend money, what to plant or what animals to buy. Staff will intervene in their problems or decisions only if the children have difficulties they cannot resolve.

CAP's handicraft projects provide another form of vocational training. The training in these centers focuses on the children's manufacturing handicraft items that they can market. This program can cater to a larger number of children.

The Farm

Niños de la Luz (Children of Light) in Venezuela offers long-term help for street children through their farm ministry. The main emphasis of this ministry is discipleship by lifestyle but also includes Bible studies, prayer and counseling.

The farm takes the children away from the lure and temptations of the street. This new environment not only provides great therapy, but also offers the children an opportunity to learn to grow food and raise animals. The children can eventually use and sell the produce they raise.

Another positive feature is the home environment, which includes "mother" and "father" figures for the children. This facilitates the children learning how to live together as a family. For practical application the "families" work together on outreach ministries, as former street children minister to other street children.

Spiritual nurture

Many street educators emphasize the intense spiritual warfare going on for the lives of street children. There is no doubt that these children need to hear the good news of Jesus' unconditional love and acceptance, his willingness to forgive and his longing to have the children become a part of his family.

Mike Watters,[2] however, reminds us, "Experience has shown us that it takes many years of prayer, discipleship and follow-up for a street child to really change and become a godly, responsible person." Such an investment of time and energy is not only a vital necessity for the children's rehabilitation, it is an invaluable hope we all can offer the world's children.

This section focuses on three strategies for promoting spiritual nurture: prayer, role modeling and camping programs.

Role modeling

Jeff Anderson[3] of Action International stresses the importance of role modeling. Anderson views role modeling as a key element in his ministry with street children in the Philippines. He suggests that what we need to model before the children includes:

◆ Compassion: this moves us from pity into action. We really care for the children.
◆ An incarnation of the gospel of Jesus Christ. This will help us to identify with their needs, feelings and aspirations.
◆ A celebration of life: play games, sing songs, perform skits, touch and hug the children, pray, tell Bible stories and serve a delicious meal. Treat their sores, cuts and wounds. The goal is to provide friendship.
◆ Engage in spiritual power encounters with our real enemy, the devil.
◆ Effective praying: we are not just providing a good time, but we are grounded and based in prayer.
◆ Team unity: we work together as a team—no lone rangers.
◆ Righteousness: our personal lives, families and ministries must have integrity.
◆ Victory in our personal lives: we also need to rise above the spiritual strongholds of the city—lust, greed, rebellion and independence.

Prayer

Esther Network International is a prayer network that teaches children how to pray. They point out that a crucial aspect of spiritual nurture for street children is teaching them to pray for themselves and for one another. Often the children do not have adults praying specifically for them and for their needs. Further, who better understands the particular problems street children are confronted with on a day by day basis than other street children? Karen Moran[4] provides some practical ways for teaching street children to pray.

Recognizing and nurturing a child's spirituality has in it the potential of releasing the church's most untapped resource of prayer power. "Let the children come to me," Jesus declared, "and do not hinder them" (Luke 18:16). That verse simply says, "Let them pray." Is that not the way we "come to him" today? Children really love to pray; please let them!

To begin with, teach the children the important place that prayer has in bringing healing in their lives. The Bible teaches us to "pray for one another, that you may be healed" (James 5:16).

Explain to the children that they have experienced many things that would help them to pray for other children. Often children think that an adult can pray a much better prayer. Encourage them with the fact that they understand and can pray more effectively for other children like them because they have experienced similar things firsthand.

Encouraging them to pray in this manner will get them "outside themselves" and not just pray for their own needs. Teach them that as they temporarily forget about their own needs and pray for others, Jesus will see to it that their own needs also are met. Stress the importance of praying from the heart and not worrying about the words they use.

To prepare their hearts for prayer, ask the children to place their hand over their hearts and speak to the Lord as follows: "Here is my heart (my thoughts and motives), Lord Jesus. If it is not clean, I ask that you cleanse it." Ask them to do the same with their hands (their actions) (Psalm 24:3-4).

Explain that they do not have to be concerned about learning to pray. Remind them of the Bible story about the little boy who only had five barley loaves and two fish to give to Jesus (John 6). But look what happened! Jesus took what the boy had and multiplied it. The results? Five thousand men PLUS women and children were fed and twelve baskets with pieces of bread were left over. God takes what we give him and multiplies it.

Train the children to pray specific, targeted prayers for their own needs and the needs of others. They can ask Jesus to:

- Provide for the physical needs of the children and their families: freedom from addiction to drugs, alcohol, hunger, poverty, disease and those caught up in the sex industry.
- Heal the emotions: healing from physical and verbal abuse, rejection and abandonment.
- Reveal how much the children are loved and accepted unconditionally by God.
- Enable other children to become a part of God's family.
- Help those that work with street children, and that the government and law officers will understand the children's situation, treating them justly.

As the children mature in their prayer life, it is important that they become global in their prayers. It is just as easy to pray and include all the children in the world that are having the same problem as you or another person. For example, if a child is praying for himself or herself and a friend to overcome fear, they can also pray for all the other children in the world that are experiencing this problem.

Prayer can bring comfort to the children's hearts. Prayer also will help them mature in their faith. Singing can be another form of prayer. Songs can lead children to worship God and to "silence the foe and the avenger" (Psalm 8:2 NIV). Scripture choruses not only lead children to worship God, they also help them learn the Word.

Camping programs

Camping programs offer a variety of opportunities for the children to receive a respite from crowded, dirty streets while providing them with physical and spiritual nurture. Two programs are highlighted in this section: Project Jabez in the Philippines and Children of Light in Venezuela.

Project Jabez

Mary Ann Anderson describes Action International's camp in the Philippines as a "refuge from the street."[5] We can ascertain why this is an apt description from the following enticing "invitation" to leave the streets behind for something far better:

> *Imagine being a street kid . . . selling candy, newspapers and flowers at a busy, smoggy intersection of a large overcrowded*

191

city. As a twelve-year-old you are always hungry and dirty. Your knowledge of drugs, gangs and prostitution makes you streetwise and tough. Your family is around but they are so busy trying to survive they can't give you the guidance, protection and love you need. Nobody really cares about you except maybe your buddies on the street.

It all seems so hopeless—one big dead end. But one day a friend invites you to a Bible camp in the country—free of charge—and he will be there. Fresh air, green grass, lots of good food three times a day, basketball, games, songs, new friends, a new set of clothes and a Bible, a medical checkup and a camp staff that loves and cares for you. Deep inside you have dreamed about something like this. Here is your opportunity for a new chance in life. You go for it!

For the first time you meet a family that loves you and you hear about a Father who won't get drunk, beat you up and kick you out of his house.

Project Jabez has all this to offer and more. The Rescue Home for street boys is located on the same property as Jabez Camp. It is offered to the street boys during camp as an alternative to returning to the streets. This large home can house up to 60 children. At the Rescue Home the boys can continue their education, learn basic skills, learn more about God and build healthy bodies in a spacious, rural environment.

Daily chores in the piggery or on the grounds help teach responsibility and allow the children to earn a little income. The area is full of mango trees, which also provide some income during mango season. During free time the boys can play basketball or soccer.

Children of Light

Niños de la Luz (Children of Light) in Caracas, Venezuela, has a multifaceted program for street children. Their camping program includes backpacking, camping and rock climbing. The fourfold purpose of their camping program is to:

1) Provide the children with an opportunity to leave their environment and spend time in God's creation;

2) Teach the children about God through nature;

3) Build self-worth and teamwork; and

4) Observe the children, providing a chance to screen them

for future placement in either their homes or church homes.

Like other organizations that conduct camps for street children, Niños de la Luz finds that their camping and other outdoor programs play a vital role in effective outreach with street children.

Outreach programs

Michael DiPaolo[6] describes an effective outreach program for street children in the following section. Covenant House's special blue vans cruise city streets throughout the night, representing a constant presence and sanctuary for those living on danger-filled city streets.

Lifeline to the street

The premise for including an aggressive outreach component to the services offered by Covenant House California is based on the recognition that many youth, whether by choice or ignorance, may not seek out services on their own. These youth may probably be the most in need.

We may generally divide these youth into two broad categories. The first group includes those runaways or "pushouts" who have recently landed on the streets, struggling to survive but not knowing where to turn. It is imperative that intervention move swiftly with this group because they can quickly become captured by the dangers of the street. The majority of youth on the street, however, are those captured ones who are hardened and distrustful of adult relationships and the social service system. These are the youth for whom the transition from streets to shelter will take a lot longer than a van ride; it will require nurturing a trusting relationship that will allow them to first believe in themselves before believing it is possible to make it off the street.

The bottom line with both groups is the vulnerability that make them urgent targets of special attention and intervention. They are in great danger and in great need. They must be sought out and reached on their territory. That is why the Covenant House van outreach program goes to Hollywood, Sunset and Santa Monica Boulevards—perhaps the nation's largest mecca of street youth—to reach out to them. Quite simply, Covenant House goes there because that's where the youth are.

In its everyday work, van outreach requires Covenant House staff to be on the streets late into the nights, sometimes as late as 4:00 or 5:00 A.M. (when it's not safe for the children to sleep). There are always at least two outreach counselors who go out driving a well-recognized, clearly marked blue van. The van is more than just a token; it is a beacon of hope amidst the despair of the street. Inside, the workers carry sandwiches and punch (hot chocolate in cooler weather) to freely distribute, no questions asked. But perhaps most important, the van provides a refuge to any youth that needs to talk or just get away for awhile. It is here in this "counseling office," in the late hours of the night, that some of the most crucial, life changing discussions occur.

The outreach program is based on a model of care called "Levels of Intervention." All of the outreach work must go at the pace set by the youth. Workers cannot push them, whether to serve their own needs or the youth's. It's their turn: they have control and the workers must respect that. The three levels of this model are:

Level 1: Lifeline support. This is immediate, concrete support (food, medical attention, crisis counseling) to youth not yet ready to accept further intervention, and so choose to live on the street. The theory at level one is based on awareness and trust. The goal is that any child knows what the workers do and feels at ease talking, "no strings attached." In many respects, the van staff become like "lifeguards." The youth know who the van workers are and how to reach them, but do so only in case of emergency. Nevertheless, there is a certain level of comfort in the back of their minds knowing that the vans are there.

Part of this lifeline is the Covenant House Nineline. This nationwide toll free hotline (1-800-999-9999) is available 24 hours a day, 7 days a week, 365 days a year for youth to call for assistance. When youth in the Los Angeles area call this number, they are immediately transferred to one of the outreach workers whose vans are equipped with mobile phones.

Level 2: Building relationships. The theory at level two is based on trust and healing. The goals are to establish and build trusting relationships, and to address the issues that brought the youth to the street and that keep the youth on the street. Consistency is crucial because this trust is a tenuous thing. It is difficult for the youth not only to begin to look at these issues, but also to open up to someone driving around all night in a blue van.

Level 3: Getting off the street. Level three begins when a youth has signaled his or her readiness to leave the streets and begin to work toward achieving other goals. Here the focus is on the decisions and concrete acts required if the youth are to make a successful transition from the street, with ongoing processing of what this transition brings. As always, the children aren't pushed because this decision necessitates that they abandon the street values with which they have become comfortable. The choice to accept an alternative is always theirs.

In van outreach, the focus is always on the process. Certain behaviors are required at each level and applied appropriately to children on the street. Being committed to the idea of "getting the children off the street" is vague, unhelpful and ultimately disappointing. It is far more productive and satisfying to practice a useful way of being with each youth as they experience the moment.

Conclusion

These examples of intervention care demonstrate that there are many creative, effective methods of providing intervention care for street children. Such care must be holistic and must have multiple levels of intervention to meet not only perceived needs, but also the children's deepest felt needs.

NOTES

1   Annette Cockburn, "Looking After Street Children: A Model Indigenous to South Africa," a paper presented at the Tenth International Congress on Child Abuse and Neglect in Kuala Lumpur, Malaysia, September 10-13, 1994.

2   Mike Watters, "Rey: New Hope—But a Hard Road!" in *Manila Heart Beat* (Vol. 10, No. 3, third quarter).

3   Jeff Anderson, Action International's Street Children's Project director in Metro Manila, the Philippines. From a paper written for this chapter.

4   Karen Moran of Esther Network International, "What About the Street Children?" an unpublished paper written for this chapter.

5   Mary Ann Anderson, "Refuge from the Street," in *Action Magazine* (Vol. 1, No. 1 12/92), pp. 8-9.

6   Michael DiPaolo, "Lifeline to the Street: The Covenant House California Outreach Program." This paper, written for this chapter, was adapted from two documents written for internal training by Covenant House: "Reaching Out to Kids on the Street: Hands and Voices on the Front Line" (Covenant House New York); and "Covenant House California Outreach: Levels of Intervention" (Covenant House California).

PART SIX:

Intervention Concerns for Street Educators

16

Caring for street educators

Cynthia Blomquist Eriksson

And let us not grow weary in well-doing, for in due season we shall reap, if we do not lose heart (Galatians 6:9).

Paul's words to the Galatians are a familiar exhortation and encouragement to a life of ministry. Ministry to street children holds amazing rewards, but also stresses and disappointments that may feel too much to bear. How does God intend his workers to avoid weariness when after months or years of work these children decide to return to their friends, steal ministry or personal property, or become victims of vigilante groups or ruthless police brutality? As we have seen in previous chapters, these children exist in a tenuous balance of risk and safety on the streets. Yet, the hearts of street educators are also caught in that balance of hope and pain, strength and freedom.

This chapter will outline the anticipated stresses of working in ministry with children on the street and suggestions for preventing and responding to these needs.

Stress and burnout

Many of us may have speculations about what the terms "stress" and "burnout" mean, but we may have little skill in recognizing them in the midst of our own lives. Some may even think, "I'm way too busy to think about burnout," or "I can't be over-stressed because someone needs to do the work here." For many those statements are completely—and unfortunately—true. The results of stress and burnout, however, can become insidious enemies to the very ministry we are pledged to serve.

Stress has a variety of impacts on both a person and a person's performance. First, stress has a negative effect on physical health. People under stress have been shown to have reduced functioning of their immune systems. Not only are they likely to develop stress-related illnesses like ulcers, headaches and colitis, but they also report more frequent general sickness like colds and influenza.

Kelly O'Donnell and Michele O'Donnell (1992) offer the following comprehensive and practical description of stress:

> Stress is the response of the entire person to various internal and external demands (stressors). . . . For example, a person may be experiencing self-doubt, grief, or physical illness (internal stressors) in conjunction with work pressures, financial difficulties, or friction with colleagues (external stressors). Put them all together and the result is the subjective experience of "stress" (p. 110).

With this definition in mind, it is clear that stressors are a natural part of life and ministry. Our daily lives are made up of any number of internal and external demands for our energy, attention and time.

When the stressors have built up to an intolerable level, a ministry worker can experience "burnout." Esther Schubert (1993), a veteran missionary and medical doctor, outlines several symptoms of burnout: negative or cynical feeling toward those one is ministering to; decrease in energy and passion for one's work; decrease in personal investment in one's work; fatigue and irritability; cynicism or sarcasm; withdrawal; physical difficulties; guilty feelings; and emptiness or emotional exhaustion.

Schubert points out that these symptoms can result from an organizational schedule or expectations that the ministry worker cannot manage. The experience of burnout can also be the product of an individual's personality that drives him or her to perform to the point of exhaustion. Some ministry workers may have personality characteristics that leave them prone to a "workaholic" lifestyle, or a relationship style that makes it difficult to say "no" or to confront unreasonable expectations.

Clearly, difficulties happen on a day-to-day basis in the ministry setting. The cumulative effect of natural stressors and the individual's decision of how to cope then determines the final experience of "stress." One particularly helpful way to cope with stressors is to anticipate them and prepare for them as much as possible.

Stress factors

The street educator can anticipate a lifestyle that requires flexibility and resiliency. Work with any child is a constant challenge of energy and creativity, as any parent would know. The energy that street educators invest in their work issues from a passion for loving and nurturing these children. To use a phrase from the U.S. military: "It's not just a job, it's an adventure!" The following suggest a few areas that may make ministry to street children an adventure with many twists and turns.

Cultural factors

Let's face it, even if you are still within the boundaries of your home country, working within the setting of the urban street child is more than likely a cross-cultural experience. One of the things that our culture provides for us is the security of expectations and structure that is "known." When we enter into an unfamiliar culture or subculture, the "unknown" itself can be a stressor. Marjory Foyle (1987) describes this process as the "loss of familiar cues" (p. 101). Without realizing it, we pick up cues from people and things around us that help us to orient to places and behaviors. Put simply, this is how we "know what's going on." In a new culture, we need to learn an entirely new set of cues. That learning process requires energy and effort that we may not have anticipated.

Workload

The street child worker enters a lifestyle of care and compassion with an intensity that is difficult to match in any other profession. A street educator is trained to develop relationships with the children living on the streets, to assess the needs of the children and to act as an advocate between the street child and service providers or law officials. This ministry role holds multiple levels of responsibility and a variety of relationships that must be maintained effectively. Add to this job description thousands of children that need this ministering hand and the street educator has a complex and overwhelming workload to face.

The workload, and decisions about how to limit one's workload, may become a significant stressor. A street worker has only a particular amount of time and energy, yet the needs are always critical and always present. A worker may find it difficult to say "no" to a child or to take appropriate personal time for rejuvenation and relaxation. You may find it helpful to remember that the word "recreation" is the idea of "re-creation." Time for re-creating life, passion and energy is a necessary, not optional, part of life.

In addition, Paul Jones (1991) emphasizes that children on the street respond to street educators who express a sincere interest and love for them. These children do not want to feel as though they are just part of a program. This individual attention and nurturing is the hallmark of a successful street ministry program. This emotional investment, however, adds significant intensity to the workload a ministry worker faces.

Imagine how much more energy it requires to listen and care, allowing your heart to be truly touched by the child. Unfortunately, when a ministry staff person begins to feel stressed and tired, the amount of energy and interest in others begins to wane. This is a vicious cycle: too high a workload may produce a decrease in sincere energy, which may mean that the children may respond to what they feel as "insincerity." It appears the answer is to make good choices about staying emotionally and spiritually rested.

Unrealistic expectations

A street worker may fight long and hard with their own sense of disappointment and depression when they cannot meet their own expectations of "fixing" or "saving" the children on the streets. Workers may tell themselves, "I should have done more" or "I could do better." Even issues of faith may mingle with painful self-accusations: "If I had prayed harder for this child, he would not have returned to the streets."

When street child caregivers have unrealistic expectations for their ministry and cannot meet those standards, depression and guilt may result. A worker that tends to be a perfectionist may experience unmet goals as deep and personal failures. When the street educator feels that the results of ministry ultimately reflect their value as a person, they have entered a vicious cycle of performance that will inevitably lead to guilt, depression and self-condemnation.

Relationships

Paul Jones (1991) emphasizes that mutual and trusting relationships between the children and a ministry's staff are the foundation for successful care. He also suggests that there are issues that have an impact on the amount of affection that adult workers can demonstrate to the children. Some workers may hold a conscious or unconscious bias against a certain ethnic group, and the adult may not provide the children of this group with the amount of physical affection they require.

The worker's natural resources of empathy and patient caring may be stretched to the limit. Knowing one's strengths and limitations will aid in determining how a worker approaches the relationships of ministry. Older workers may find the required physical play to establish a connection with the children exhausting. Younger workers may be more effective in the front-lines of care, establishing the early connections with children through fun and games.

Those workers with natural gifts of listening and encouragement could offer the priceless nurturing that these children need. Jones (1991) reminds us that the children deserve (and require) relationship-focus, not project-focus. Therefore, the ministry worker will need to invest a tremendous amount of time and patience in the lives of these children, perhaps even at the expense of the project.

Attachment and emotional involvement

A ministry that is so predominantly based on relationship holds the risks of emotional over-involvement and distress. Paul Jones writes in response to his years of working with street children in Vietnam and Bangladesh:

> When such [mutual and trusting] relationships are founded, the children often tend to "overreact" to the worker, sometimes with almost obsessive affection and openness. Naturally, the project worker can have great influence on the child's life at this point, especially in terms of helping the child find a saving relationship with Christ (1991:5).

While these relationships become priceless tools of ministry and change, the child's dependence and "obsessive affection" may overwhelm a street educator. It is extremely important that each staff member has the freedom to spend time by themselves or with a valued friend in order to "recharge." Even parents need time apart from their children to develop their own emotional support system.

Staff members may be faced with difficult decisions regarding care for a child with a special bond. Take time to discuss these situations with fellow team members. Keep other staff involved in your relationship with the child. It is a delicate balance to invest your heart in the life of the child, while still maintaining a space where God can meet you and the child as individuals. You may be in danger of overwhelmed boundaries if you believe that you are the only one that can help a child. While you may have the closest relationship with them, God can be creative in how he ministers to these children.

Outside forces

Those who have been working with street children may be aware of the stress associated with negative community reaction to ministry with children rejected by society. The response can range from simple unpopularity in the community and difficulty finding supportive neighbors, to threats and actual physical violence. The children often are of little value to the community. They are sometimes viewed as nuisances to be disposed of. Therefore, those who have invested their lives in caring for such children may seem strange and undesirable or even seen as a threat.

Covenant House and Childhope have been actively speaking out against human rights violations against street children. Unfortunately, there have already been documented cases of abductions and threats against street educators and children's workers. Amnesty International reports that in January 1992 three former staff of the Covenant House in Guatemala left their country after a series of death threats, abductions, harassment and a rape (Amnesty International Index, 1992). Amnesty International and Covenant House also report at least one murder of a staff person by a police agent, also in Guatemala (Amnesty International: Guatemala, July 1990).

We cannot forget the outside forces of spiritual warfare. Ministering to these precious children on the streets puts a worker on the front-lines of pain and evil. The enemy certainly delights in the broken lives, addictions, treachery and hopelessness that infiltrate life on urban streets. We cannot overemphasize the amount of emotional and spiritual energy that is required in simply facing all this evil. In addition, many believe that the work of very personal evil, such as satanic worship and witchcraft, is active across national and ethnic boundaries. Abandoned or runaway children may be targets for these groups.

Prevention and intervention

Knowing what to expect offers some comfort in any journey or adventure. Preventive measures can be powerful, even if it includes an action as simple as bringing an umbrella on a walk when it looks as if it may rain. The following suggestions provide tools for preventing or responding to a variety of ministry stressors.

Personal reflection

Jeff Anderson (1995) suggests keeping a journal of your successes and failures. The mistakes offer invaluable insight for continued growth. In addition, the process of writing and reflecting will prepare you to share your thoughts with other workers and leaders. A journal may also be an important resource to keep track of the points of progress and joy you experience along the way. Often in working with people the results are not quick to surface or obvious.

Create a social support network

Social support is one of the most important areas of care for the stresses of ministry. No one should have to bear the burden of this intense ministry all by themselves. Have a planned time to "process" with ministry team members and colleagues, not as an opportunity to do ministry strategizing, but to emphasize the relationships within the team. During this sharing, the group should address any team conflict, encourage one another when someone is feeling down or isolated and offer assistance when a team member feels overwhelmed. The street educator team will need to feel that this dialogue happens in a safe environment. Each leader and team member deserves a place to express their anger, frustration, disappointment, fears and inadequacies without the concern that he or she will be judged or challenged. Expressing these feelings allows the street educator to find a renewed perspective on the depth of these emotions and where the source of these reactions lies.

One should also remember individual differences in how each team member responds to the group. If it is a large team, some members may feel uncomfortable sharing their painful emotions. Smaller groups or one-on-one relationships (like prayer partners) can be additional support for those that do not feel as comfortable in the larger group setting. I would not use smaller groups as an option to the team setting, due to the need to develop healthy team relationships.

In addition, relationships with people in the community (national or expatriate) who are not directly working with street children can offer an invaluable place to relieve some internal pressure and stress.

Be reasonable about your workload

Practice the art of setting limits, or boundaries. Each street educator or ministry worker has a particular limit of time, energy, resources and competencies. To be good stewards of all those gifts, team members should encourage one another to make wise choices regarding the use of those resources. In addition, team members should not be made to feel guilty if they cannot complete a project, or if they feel limited in their competencies. Each person has particular skills and gifts that can be invested in the lives of these children.

Make decisions in advance about time to relax and "re-create." One minister I worked with in the U.S.A. reported that he followed a simple schedule for his day. He broke each of his five "working" days into three parts: morning, afternoon and evening. He made the commitment to himself and his family that each day one of the "parts" would be reserved for family and personal time. When evening meetings were scheduled, he made certain that he reserved some morning or afternoon time for family interaction and personal necessities. This way he maintained the space he and his family needed for healthy service and ministry.

Be prepared for difficulties

Plan strategies on how you or your team will deal with threats or traumatic events. Know ahead of time where the nearest place of safety is. Clarify an evacuation plan to execute in the event of any kind of emergency. Make connections with leaders in the community who support your ministry.

In addition, take the time to talk through any upsetting experiences with a co-worker. Team leaders may also conduct a debriefing session where each team member has an opportunity to share his or her emotional responses to a painful event that the entire team has experienced. This time for group support may prove invaluable in preventing heartaches from festering and becoming a crippling emotional wound.

An investment of life

Encourage ministry staff to appreciate the ways that their gifts and care have an impact on the lives of the children in the streets. Also, the gifts and care of the children have an impact on the lives of the street educators. One of the ways that God can truly deepen our sense of his work in the world is when we allow him to use those we are ministering to to minister to us. What a gift to these children, for them to see how they make the life of the street educator a deeper, richer place!

It is in the face of this hope, joy and growth, even in desperate circumstances, that Christ renews and invigorates. Perhaps this is Paul's intention to "not grow weary" (Galatians 6:9). As we minister with our knowledge, gifts or limitations, and let others minister to us as well, the Lord renews our lives and carries us graciously through our commitment of care and sacrifice.

REFERENCES

Amnesty International. Guatemala, 1990.

Amnesty International. *Guatemala: Street children.* Amnesty International Index: AMR 34/24/92, 1992, p. 10.

Anderson, Jeff. *Crisis on the Streets.* Manila: Philippines, 1995, p. 3.

Foyle, Marjory. *Overcoming Missionary Stress.* Wheaton: Evangelical Missions Information Service, 1987.

Jones, Paul. "Ministering to Street Children," in *Together*, 32:1991, pp. 3-5.

O'Donnell, Kelly and Michele O'Donnell. "Understanding and managing stress," in *Missionary Care: Counting the Cost for World Evangelization*, Kelly O'Donnell, ed. Pasadena: William Carey Library, 1992, pp. 110-132.

Schubert, Esther. *What Missionaries Need to Know About Burnout and Depression.* New Castle: Olive Branch Publications, 1993.

17

Exploring ethical issues

David High

On the surface, intervening in the life of a street child may seem to be an easy and simple thing to do. Upon entering this line of work, however, tough questions such as, "What is the right thing to do?" start to arise. For example, a young girl tells a social worker that she wants to leave the streets. Immediately, questions are formulated: Who is the legal guardian of the child? What is the best rehabilitation method for the child? What discipline can be administered to the child? And so on.

Likewise, similar types of questions occur when opening a children's home. For example, a Brazilian woman with a very compassionate heart opens her home to the street children of her city. She has no acceptance policy for the new home and takes in any child who has been abandoned, because she cannot stand the thought of turning away a needy child. Very quickly she starts to experience trouble caring for all the children because she has run out of resources and space. She continues to take in additional children, however, because she rationalizes that at least they are off the streets and someone cares for them.

Before long the health conditions in the home become deplorable and the neighbors file complaints with the city. Recognizing there is a problem, the city closes down the woman's orphanage. The question as to how many children the woman could effectively care for is a relevant ethical question.

There are other ethical questions: What will the standards of discipline be? How is the necessary discipline going to be administered? What standard of living is going to be maintained? Questions on similar issues arise in caring for abandoned children. How these ethical questions are answered will determine the effectiveness and integrity of the intervention work. Expect to face questions concerning what is the right or wrong thing to do. Such evaluation is an integral part of preparing to work with street children.

Since ethics deals with what is "good" and "bad" in human conduct, ethical issues have to do with what is the "right" or "the morally correct" action to take in a certain situation. Because the number of situations are endless, the issues presented here are intended only to create thought for preparation purposes. Readiness is important when ethical issues arise as decision-making time usually is limited.

This chapter is not written to provide all the answers to every ethical issue concerning a ministry with street children, but to focus on the need to be prepared for these types of issues.

Proper use of donated funds

Probably the primary ethical concern in the intervention work of street children is the proper and honest gain and use of donated funds. Examples in recent years of organizations and ministries using large percentages of donated funds for advertisement, administrative costs or personal gain have raised serious ethical concerns among governments and communities.

Organizations raising money for one reason and spending it for another also have appeared to be on the rise. Since the designation of many donations is not specified, an ethical issue arises regarding the obligation of determining how to spend that donation. Eventually, someone must decide if a donation will go toward meeting the overhead financial needs of the ministry or for actual intervention needs.

Ideally, a group of individuals, such as a board of directors, must oversee the expenditure of donated funds. Using such a board, however, can often be frustrating for the director of a home or ministry because of the differences in opinions as to what is the most pressing need at the time.

Often ethical issues can arise if an organization does not practice "disclosive" financial management. At the bare minimum, a written statement should be given to a donor explaining how the funds were used. Likewise, public disclosure of how funds are being spent should be standard practice.

Child abuse

Another major ethical question arises when working with abandoned children: Where is the fine line between caring for and mistreating a child? Where do the rights of children stop and the rights of those trying to provide care begin? When does one decide that more harm than help is being accomplished?

Often workers never give consideration to the rights or interests of the child because they rationalize that their actions are acceptable. After all, they know they are trying to help the child; what harm could be done? Questions dealing with standards of living and rules about discipline must be given consideration. Knowing customs, cultures and laws concerning these types of issues is necessary for anyone wanting to work with street children.

Exploiting a child

Distinguishing between exploiting a child and helping a child is yet another ethical issue commonly experienced among those who work with street children. Real ethical questions arise about when, how and why it is acceptable to use a child's condition or situation for marketing purposes to raise funds to provide care for the child.

Placing yourself in the child's situation may make the issue clearer. Would you like to have a picture of your dirty face and human misery held up for the whole world to see? Is it right to destroy the human dignity of a child so that administrative workers can be paid? Even receiving a child's permission to use his photograph does not necessarily make it right to use the picture.

Usually very little thought is given to this matter, because people rationalize that the child cannot be helped unless funds are raised by this method. But depriving children of human dignity and prostituting their situation for a good cause does not remove the ethical issues involved. An organization must establish policies and guidelines concerning how they will use a child's story.

Playing God

Intervention workers often find themselves in dire situations with limited resources. At these times, the worker has to decide who receives help and who does not. Is it best to help a few well, or many poorly? What is best for a particular child? Should the child be returned to abusive parents, put in a children's home or put up for adoption? When is it necessary to remove a child from a home for the sake of the other children? What standard of living does one maintain for one's own family versus the standard provided for the children you are trying to help? Determining the answers to such questions is very difficult. Care in considering the needs and desires of everyone involved is very important in making the right decision.

Knowing the law

It is important to know the laws governing child care. Countries differ in regulations on the rights of children and the standard of care that is expected. Sometimes obeying these regulations is difficult because they seem to be a waste of time and resources. However, obeying the laws is vital in maintaining the integrity of any intervention work.

Maintaining integrity

The integrity of a ministry will depend on the everyday decisions made by each worker. Keeping financial matters public, formulating principles for the ministry, being honest in obeying all the legal statutes and placing intervention work under the review of others are all good methods to ensure that integrity is maintained in a ministry.

Guidelines to follow to ensure that a ministry maintains its integrity are:

1) Have a board of directors oversee the work.

2) Have a set of biblical principles as the foundation for the ministry.
3) Always be honest and do not look for ways to take short cuts.
4) Disclose all financial dealings.
5) Always have the interest of the child in mind when making decisions concerning the child.
6) Abide by the laws of the country.
7) Treat others with respect and with fairness.

The above guidelines will help in most situations. But unending new ethical dilemmas can arise. How should you approach them? A general guideline for reaching the right resolution to every issue makes "love-mastered" thinking and "love-mastered" activity the basis for each decision. Christ-centered love is the basis for the highest of all ethical conceptions. There is no law against love. Love will always fulfill the law. If love is the test of our lives, then we will not lie, we will not be selfish, we will not want our own way, we will not slander, we will not steal, we will not hate and we will care for children in the proper manner.

Concerning any social problem dealing with the care of street children, the right resolution will be found if our hearts and minds are love-mastered. Carefully checking the basis for our decisions will help us know if we are doing the right thing.

PART SEVEN:

Child Advocacy Issues

18

Changing society's attitudes

David High

The most prevalent community-held attitudes toward abandoned children are hostility and fear. Street children often steal, prostitute themselves or beg to survive. They are easy prey for the drug dealers, pimps and thief bosses who use the children to do their "dirty work." Because street children are used in this manner, they become associated with these street-related problems. Negative attitudes toward street children develop quickly and are widespread where they congregate.

Workers trying to intervene on behalf of street children must address these attitudes and face the challenge of overcoming them. Much of the long-term achievements of intervention work depends on successfully changing the community's attitudes toward these children. Change requires the community to perceive the children as destitute human beings with great needs instead of out-of-control adolescent criminals.

To change the community's opinion of these children, there must first be a radical change in the children's behavior. The visibility of this change must be great enough to convince those who hold prejudices against street children to view them in a whole new light.

216

The following suggestions are presented to assist intervention workers with the task of determining a community's
attitudes toward street children and what possibilities are available to help change existing prejudices.

Uncovering existing attitudes

One of the first tasks that must be considered when establishing a new intervention program for street children is uncovering the community's existing attitudes toward the children or
a new work. Determine not only what the prejudices are, but
who has them.

Do not be surprised to discover a very strong intolerance
toward street children from local merchants and the general
population. For example, the murder of eight street children at
the Candelaria Cathedral in downtown Rio de Janeiro in February 1994 caused a great outcry in the world press. Local opinion toward the murders, however, was quite different. Many
local merchants called a police hotline following the announce-
ment of the murders to state how pleased they were that this
action had been taken. Public officials even went on television
to point out the need to rid the streets of such nuisances and
criminals. The attitude toward these children was simply that
these were not human beings, but animals that should be
slaughtered for the sake of the community.

Attempting to start interventions in such an environment
is dangerous, exhausting and time consuming. But understanding the attitudes that exist and why they exist is an important key to having a successful project to help the children.

Likewise, many already existing street projects and transi-
tional homes have ongoing problems with the community
because of misunderstanding or poor communication. A few
rumors can very quickly bring good work to a sudden halt.
Open the channels of communication between the intervention
work and the community as soon as possible and take care to
maintain them.

One method used to discover prejudices toward abandoned children is taking informal community attitude surveys.
The objective of these surveys should be to identify the root
causes of existing opinions. Start by trying to identify who has
the most interaction with the children and who is the most

affected by the street children's presence. Researching local papers and news media broadcasts are also good sources for determining a community's attitude. Speaking with neighbors concerning their feelings about your ministry's moving into their community is very important. If possible, develop a history of the town or community's street children concerns to enable you to understand the duration and severity of the problem.

Another effective method of uncovering the existing attitudes toward street children is to speak with the children themselves. The children have discovered very quickly how others view them. Taking the time to listen to how they have to live begins the interaction process necessary to gain the children's trust.

A third source for uncovering existing attitudes toward abandoned children is the social workers already involved in this type of work. These individuals are a great resource and will probably give the best understanding of how the local community feels about these children.

You cannot change opinions in a community until you understand why these attitudes exist. If a community is concerned that the project will become a magnet for drawing more dangerous children into the community, take steps to prevent such a reality or perception. Only by taking the time to build bridges of trust and communication can you expect to distance a work from negative opinions.

Opening the lines of communication

Once you have a clear understanding of the existing opinions and have identified their root causes, you must open lines of communication within the community. Since most negative attitudes concerning street children are formed by fear and mistrust, develop strategies for overcoming fear by building trust.

Many tools and resources are available for use in educating the people and promoting your work. A few examples include pamphlets, articles in the local newspaper, speaking at community gatherings, holding an "open house" or having a dedication service for the work. You must be careful, however, not to "overdo it." Pressing too hard can result in the opposite effect, and the work may be singled out as being from outside the community instead of being a part of the community.

Educating the public through the local press may be a means of changing a community's understanding of street children. One of the most impressive examples of this method can be found in Nairobi, where local newspapers were used to educate and create sympathy for the city's street children. Having a wide range of support, including business and government leaders, helps bring tremendous attention to the issue.

Another avenue for building communication and trust within a community is through local churches and professional organizations. Local churches very often provide support for a new work and are centers where caring adults will listen to the needs of these children. Prayer is probably the most important need of a new work and it is vital to have the prayer support of a local church.

Also important is the understanding that bringing these children into the church can lead to problems within the church, causing the prejudices of some church members to sur-face. Nevertheless, churches remain one of the best resources to use in building trust within a community.

Another significant approach for building trust within a community is through local government officials and commu-nity leaders. The leaders may be able to give you some under-standing as to why the problem exists and how you can be involved in a solution.

It is also very important to spend time with the people of the community. Listening to the neighbors' complaints and concerns is the key to the acceptance of an intervention work by the members of a community. Community awareness of the intervention's purpose and the operational methods used in executing the intervention will help remove the potential for rumor and false accusations to arise. Having events such as an open house or special projects to help the community's health or environment are vital ways of improving integrity and developing trust.

Having a long-term commitment is very important in cre-ating an atmosphere of trust in the community. Understanding that you genuinely care for their community and that you have made a long-term commitment to your work will help the com-munity members to see you as part of their community, not as an outsider. Adopting their customs and learning their language will also carry a lot of weight.

Finally, do not undervalue the role of prayer when trying to change a community's attitude toward and acceptance of street children. The spiritual warfare that is at the heart of this problem can only be fought with prayer. Set aside time each day to pray that these children will be used to touch hearts in the community for Christ.

Determining a plan of action

Developing strategies to involve the community in a new work is an excellent way to develop trust and open the lines of communication. Action strategies for achieving goals, whether simple or complex, are necessary. Include the need to respect the rights and opinions of others in your strategy planning. Plan to listen to what others have to say, even if they offer different views. Aim to be as tolerant with differences as possible. Try to identify the reasons for people's attitudes and feelings, devising methods to bring about needed change.

Finally, plan to expose the senselessness of hate while showing the real potential and changes possible in the children's lives. Bring moral pressure to bear on those who are using and abusing street children.

19

Becoming a voice
for the children

Phyllis Kilbourn

They labor in factories and fields until their hands are gnarled and their backs bent. They sell their bodies in the alleyways of Recife and Beirut and Nairobi until they are haggard or dead from AIDS. They wander homeless in the streets of Naples and Khartoum and New York City, surviving by begging and thieving. They die by the thousands every day, of easily preventable diseases like measles and whooping cough. They are the world's disadvantaged children. If present trends continue, more than 100 million youngsters will die, most of them unnecessarily, of illness and malnutrition or both during the 1990s. Their neglect by governments preoccupied with politics, guns and national debt leads child-care workers the world over to ask the plaintive question: Does anyone care?[1]

Who does care for the tragic plight of children worldwide—especially those children who have been cut off from the adults who should be loving and nurturing them? Perhaps a more relevant question would be, "Whose responsibility is it to care for the children?" Can we simply relegate ownership of the problem to governments and social agencies? What responsibilities, if any, does the Christian community have?

Perhaps the first step toward the solution for the children's plight is, as James Beaunaux suggests, "for the Christian world community to recognize that all of us can have a part."[2] We not only can but must own the problem and seek for solutions. We will, however, only do that when we are responding rightly to God's commands, responding in ways that cause the Christian community to assume responsibility for the welfare of the world's children.

One command to which we can all actively respond is referred to in many Scripture passages: "Speak up for those who cannot speak for themselves, for the rights of all who are destitute. Speak up and judge fairly; defend the rights of the poor and needy" (Proverbs 31:8-9 NIV).

Street children fall into the category of "those who cannot speak for themselves": they have no political power, cannot vote and their opinions carry little, if any, weight with governments. They are totally dependent on adults to act in their best interests and to protect them, adults who are willing to become their voice, or advocate. An advocate signifies that someone is pleading on behalf of another person's cause.

In Old Testament culture, the king of Israel was commanded to be a voice for those who could not speak for themselves or who needed someone to defend their rights. The king was to represent God as the defender of the poor and needy. Then, as now, it could be said that, "The true test of a civilization is how well it protects its vulnerable and how well it safeguards its future; children are both its vulnerable and its future.[3]

Leaders today still have the responsibility of being a voice for the needy, but far too often they remain silent; they have abdicated that obligation. Often governments are caught violating street children's rights rather than ensuring that those rights are fully protected. Governments have the means and knowledge to protect children from abuse and exploitation; it is simply not a high-item priority on their agendas.

With many governments failing in their responsibility to be a voice for the children, the Christian community must assume responsibilities for being that voice in new, active and far-reaching ways. They must become a united voice that forcefully reminds governments, communities and the church of their responsibilities for the welfare of children, stirring the world's conscience through advocacy and legislation.

A philosophy of advocacy

Kanlungan sa Erma is a refuge for street children in the Philippines. *Kanlungan*, a Tagalog word, means "refuge" or "sanctuary," *sa* means "in," and *Erma* is a nickname for the adjoining red-light districts of metropolitan Manila. Thus, *Kanlungan sa Erma* is a place of refuge in a "hellish district of exploitation."[4]

Kanlungan's underlying philosophy forms a solid foundation and set of convictions to guide and inspire the work of advocacy on behalf of street children. Without internalizing these convictions, we will not be motivated to dedicate our time and efforts to becoming the much-needed voice for children trapped by the streets. *Kanlungan* affirms the belief:

◆ That every child is a precious gift from God and his or her nurture and total development must be society's concern;

◆ In the innate dignity and worth of a child and his or her capacity for change and development;

◆ That each child has a right to belong to a family, which has the primary responsibility to provide for the total physical, social, material and spiritual development of the child;

◆ That society has the obligation to assist and strengthen the family. In the absence of a family, there is a need for shelter and residential training to help the child become aware of his or her personal worth and develop his or her full potential; and

◆ That a large number of children in our country have to work because poverty pressures them to go out to the streets to earn a living for themselves and their families. Thus, they must be provided access to opportunities for decent work.

223

Advocate for what?

Through carefully examining the above convictions, along with firsthand knowledge of the children's street-life, we can derive a list of issues vital to advocacy. Such a list should include:

- ◆ Improving community attitudes toward street children and reducing discrimination against them.
- ◆ Creating a greater public awareness and understanding of the children's problems.
- ◆ Safeguarding the rights of street children as outlined in the "United Nations Convention on the Rights of the Child," including the rights to receive adequate food, shelter, health care, educational and vocational opportunities, criminal justice, life, love and respect.
- ◆ Recognizing and tapping into sources of funding and other resources to meet the children's basic needs.
- ◆ Influencing government policy and practice at all levels: enforcement of laws regarding children's rights and advocating for legislative action when needed laws have not been enacted.
- ◆ Identifying obstacles to change and planning strategies to remove those obstacles.
- ◆ Lobbying for policies, reforms and changes, such as the need to dignify and improve the work situations of street children.
- ◆ Protesting against those who are exploiting the children: drug dealers, merchants.
- ◆ Enactment of laws that prohibit brutality against children, such as being tortured, burned, exploited, maimed, sold into slavery, forced into prostitution and murdered.
- ◆ Supporting and strengthening the efforts of families to provide adequately for their children—work-related issues, assistance programs and, where needed, child care.
- ◆ Convincing courts to cease their harsh treatment of children who often are defined as criminals simply by their presence on the streets.
- ◆ Advocating for the need of family or domestic courts, ver-

sus criminal courts, to address the children's street-related problems.

To gain firsthand knowledge of advocacy needs, we must identify with the children and become immersed in their local communities. This will include home visits and involvement in local politics and the justice system. These activities will provide further significant indicators of advocacy issues unique to your project and neighborhood.

Effective methods

As you develop an awareness and understanding of the community, along with its problems and resources, the most effective methods for advocacy in a particular area will become evident. Successful methods include:

- Raising public awareness through such means as posters, educative methods, rallies, peaceful demonstrations, mobile theater groups (including children's theater groups), marches;
- Initiating boycotts (such as against those supplying glue to children or shopkeepers who mistreat children);
- Provoking debate and discussion through the media (newspapers, newsletters and other print media, radio, television, videos) about children's problems and issues; and
- Seeking reforms through political lobbying and letter-writing campaigns.

Some advocates believe that street children themselves can be a powerful voice in bringing their situations before the public. While this may be true, some precautions must be heeded. Amnesty International repeatedly voices concern for street children's safety when their situations are exposed. Indications are that those who press for inquiries into violations against street children and street children who have made declarations about abuses they have suffered or witnessed may be in danger of reprisals.

Incidents of reprisals by police and government officials have been documented including harassment, brutal beatings, intimidation and even murder. Amnesty International is calling for guarantees for the children's security, but the call mainly seems to go unheeded. *Pulse* illustrates this truth with a tragic account of a child activist's death:

> Igbal Masih, a globe-trotting 12-year-old Christian activist against forced child labor, was shot dead on Easter in his home village of Muritke, Pakistan. Igbal, who suffered "psycho-social dwarfism" due to the rigors of factory life, had received numerous death threats from the company's powerful carpet-weaving industry after shutting down dozens of establishments.[5]

Advocates must attempt to provide anonymity and safety for the children they involve in advocacy.

Becoming a voice

To become a voice for street children we must first examine our attitudes toward them. Is our attitude one of exasperation ("they are getting what they deserve") or do we truly hold to a biblical view of the worth and value of all children as expressed in *Kanlungan*'s philosophy? When our attitudes are biblically based, we consider it a God-given privilege to be a voice for these children. Advocating for rights that would make them recipients of a more loving, productive and hopefilled life is one way to fulfill God's command to "love one another."

Do we perceive the task as a God-ordained responsibility? Understanding the task in this way will enable us to remain faithful when the going gets tough—when opposition, threats and defeats seem to prevail.

Understanding the urgency of our task also will goad us into staying on track. Peter Tacon, UNICEF's long-time street child expert, warns:

> If you don't care about [children], you're condemning the world to a legacy of real human degradation, human deprivation. If you don't care about kids, then you don't care about the future. You're tossing away a precious resource. There's a tremendous human cost that will result from our not caring. One question is, Why should you care? The other question is, What happens if you don't?[6]

To be an effective voice, we must be aware of the rights accorded children by local governments and the international community. Most governments have rules that protect children's rights, even though the rules are not enforced. International documents on the rights of children, most notably the United Nations' Convention on the Rights of the Child, can become powerful weapons for advocacy.

Our ultimate goal

The longing for an arbitrator, an advocate, is an important motif in the book of Job. In chapter five, Eliphaz describes how he would appeal to God if he were in Job's situation. Verse 16 states the reason for his appeal: "So the poor have hope, and injustice shuts its mouth" (NIV). We could express our ultimate goal for advocacy on behalf of children with these same words.

We can never fully realize this ideal; injustice will always abound in the world. The goal, however, is worthy of keeping sharply in focus and striving toward as we become actively engaged in advocacy on behalf of the world's children, their communities and families. Although we will not see "injustice shut its mouth" totally, we can always discover multiple avenues for providing what is needed to bring hope to the poor children living and working on the world's streets.

NOTES

1   "Children without Hope," in *Time International* (October 1, 1990). Quoted in *Esperanza* (Volume 3, June 1991), p. 7.

2   James Beaunaux, "Children at Risk," in *Evangelical Missions Quarterly* (October 1993), p. 377.

3   UNICEF, *The State of the World's Children* (1989).

4   Consuelo M. Balbero, "Philippines: A Refuge Amid Exploitation," in *Together* (October-December 1991), pp. 12-13.

5   *Pulse* (May 26, 1995), p. 6.

6   Graeme Irvine, "Abandoned Children: The Most Marginalized," in *Together* (October-December 1991), p. 1.

PART EIGHT:

Concluding Reflection

20

Treasures, not trash!

Doug Nichols

Silent Cry

I'm one of the thousands
Of needy children in Brazil.
Without dreams, I live the present.
My life is such a sad story,
Without dreams, tales or enchantments.
I mean a suffering people,
That dies due to lack of bread.
I give you my little heart and ask you,
"Give me your love.
Come and take part in this story,
Take part in the solution.
This is transforming stone into bread;
It's overflowing the desert
With living water."

A little heart
Desirous for love, how many times
I've been crying and shouting?

But nobody listens;
I'm a silent cry.

—Sueli Duarte Costa e Melo, World Vision Brazil

One hundred million extremely underprivileged street children struggle to survive in today's cities, according to United Nations estimates. One hundred million! Such an enormous figure staggers our imaginations. Let us put it another way. If you counted one street child per second, that would be 60 each minute, 3,600 in one hour or 86,400 in one twenty-four hour day. It would take over 23 days to count to two million. To count all 100 million of the world's street children would take over 1,157 days or three years and two months.

Some government leaders say the world's street children will be the number one problem in the twenty-first century. The "mindset" of cultures toward these children is causing millions of them to struggle with problems stemming from being devalued, disrespected, used as bargaining chips and pawns or murdered in police sweeps. How should we react and respond to this enormous problem?

Society says, "Trash them!"

Chapter one listed some of the name tags society ascribes to these precious children who have been created in the image of God: nasty kids, vermin, garbage, castoffs, worthless, trash. Some communities even espouse the notion of doing society a favor by ridding the streets of these children. "If we let them grow up," the thinking goes, "they will become criminals—a blight on our society."

Such attitudes lead policemen (and others) to "moonlight" by contracting to kill street children. Amnesty International reports that disturbing research by Brazilian organizations has shown that street children and adolescents are increasingly falling victim to death squads. In the past five years there has been an alarming increase in activity by these squads in many Brazilian cities. Ordered street sweeps are always a terrifying threat to the children.

Recognize their worth

Gonzalo Arango,[1] in a meditation in his book *Lament for Desquite*, ponders a gripping question that we, as a church family, also must seriously contemplate—both personally and corporately:

I asked over his grave that was dug in the side of the mountain, "Isn't there some way that Colombia, instead of killing her children, can make them worthy of living?"

What is our answer? Is there no way for the church, having the greatest and most powerful resources, to "make" these children worthy of living? The focus of all our efforts should be to be used by the Lord Jesus in making street children "worthy of living."

Jesus said, "Let the children come to me, and do not hinder them" (Matthew 19:14). Do we hinder the children by not including them in our mission strategies? Children—referred to as the largest unreached people's group—are often bypassed by most church planting efforts. Like Jesus' disciples, many church planters are adult-driven in their mission philosophy, rarely including children in their strategies.

We cannot, however, relegate this Herculean ministry only to those with a natural affinity and love for children. Church and mission leaders need to pray and plan aggressively to reach children, not push the responsibility on a few children's workers. All of us can—and must—play an active part in extending the love of Jesus to these children.

Identify with their pain

In reaching out, however, we must not confuse pity with compassion. Michael Christensen makes an important distinction between these two words:

> With pity we keep our distance, our altitude, our sense of elevation. Compassion, on the other hand, is "suffering with." It's similar to the word "companion," which means "a person who shares one's bread," only in this case we share not just bread but passion—pain, isolation, social disregard and political disdain. Compassion is invasive, it will not leave us our privacy.[2]

Children of the streets need our compassion, not our pity. We need to identify with their pain, their sense of abandonment, degradation, loss of purpose and lack of hope for a meaningful future. We need to make it easy for these children to respond to the gospel of Christ.

Polish the jewels

Without providing care for the children's physical needs, there is usually no opportunity to communicate with street children. Although they are starving for both physical and spiritual bread, we must meet their physical needs first. Without this help no effective opportunities will open to present spiritual food.

This fact was demonstrated vividly when I made a recent visit to Mexico. I visited locations where Action International Ministry's team visits regularly in outreach to street children. At one location, five of us slid down a muddy bank to a storm drain near a busy expressway. I got down on my knees beside the team leader, Jesus Gutierrez, and peered into the dark, horizontal tunnel. In a loud voice Jesus called into the tunnel, announcing our arrival to anyone sleeping in the drain. Presently a young man of 18 crawled out, then a 14-year-old girl followed. Soon four filthy youth sat before us, half-consciously listening as we shared the gospel.

The children found it very difficult to concentrate on the Good News we had come to share. Itchy from vermin, filthy, fearful and hungry, they continually looked around in case the police were nearby. In my heart I knew if we provided a camp or other facility for these children they wouldn't have these problems. In a loving, safe environment they would experience what all children should experience: freedom from fear, clean bodies and full stomachs. Then they would begin to understand and comprehend the truth of the gospel. This effective evangelism would only be possible after we first meet the children's physical needs.

People who work with neglected, abandoned street children have found that being unwanted is one of the children's greatest hurts. They long to be loved, to be accepted and respected—in other words, to be *someone*. Has our fountain of love dried up? Do we have no love to shower on these children?

Redeem the treasures

The Lord is building his church and has asked us to go into *all* the world to preach the gospel and disciple people into the fellowship of a local church. We, therefore, must trust him to show us his plan for bringing street children and their families into the church. It can be done; we must not fail!

Recently I read of Gladys Aylward's harrowing journey out of war-torn Yangcheng with more than one hundred orphaned children. During the journey she grappled with despair. After passing a sleepless night, she faced the morning with no hope of reaching safety. A 13-year-old girl in the group reminded her of their much loved story of Moses and the Israelites crossing the Red Sea. "But I am not Moses," Gladys cried in desperation. "Of course you are not," the girl said, "but Jehovah is still God!"[3]

Don Miller of Compassion International[4] gives four basic reasons why evangelism among "the smaller half of the world" is so important:

1) *Scriptural*: God said of the Ten Commandments, "Impress them on your children." Ministry to children is central to the Ten Commandments.

2) *Statistical*: Child evangelism is important because children are the bulk of the world's population.

3) *Sociological*: Children play important roles in society—both positive as well as negative. The majority of the world's 100 million street children are becoming a plague to society and must be reached with the gospel.

4) *Strategic*: By reaching children we can reach the whole society.

Miller added: "I think we ought to minister to children because they are worthy of ministry, rather than to look at children as a vehicle to get to somebody else. That's a little manipulative. . . . We can do both in a single ministry. We . . . minister to children because they are worthy of ministry and a natural fallout in which we will rejoice is that they will have an influence on the rest of society."

Give them hope

These millions of children will only have their cry for love and hope fulfilled if the church seriously embraces the challenge of making ministry to them much more central to its task. If the church fails to accept its biblically-appointed mission it, too, could very well experience a sense of hopelessness through the profound loss of many priceless, God-given treasures.

Most of us would affirm that the church is the only instrument through which real hope can be provided for the world's hurting children. But are we willing to make the needed sacrifice—personally and corporately—to be that instrument of hope?

Street children are worthy of our ministry. May we respond redemptively and accept the challenge before us, going all out to reach the millions of street children to the glory of God. Our plans for reaching these children should be so big that if they fail, only we get the blame; but if they succeed, only God gets the glory! The children the world calls "nobodies, rats, disposable ones, the scum of society" are not trash, but special God-given treasures!

NOTES

1   Arango Gonzalo, *Elegia A Desquite,* (Cinep, 1990). Quoted in "Children at Risk" by James Beaunaux in *Evangelical Missions Quarterly* (October 23, 1993), p. 27.

2   Michael J. Christensen, "You Did it unto Me," in *Herald of Holiness* (173, No. 23, December 1, 1984), p. 5.

3   Ray Beeson, *The Hidden Price of Greatness* (Wheaton: Tyndale Publishers, 1991), pp. 141-142.

4   Don Miller, Compassion International. From a presentation given at an EFMA conference in 1993.

APPENDIXES

Appendix A:
Children helping children[1]

Clare Hanbury

The idea

Many thousands of children live or work on the streets. Even those children who have little contact with their home or a school have close contacts with other children. Most children look for comfort and support from their friends. Children can help to strengthen and build good relationships in their families and in the community. They can learn to respect one another and learn ways of improving their own health and that of others.

Understanding children who live or work on the streets

There are many reasons why children live or work on the street. Poverty and split families are the main ones. Children who live or work on the street:

- may have no home;
- may not want to live at home;
- may be sent out of the home by their parents to sell things or to beg;
- may be trying to help their families get money.

Karanja

    Karanja's mother left home. His father's new "wife" moved in.
    She was unkind to Karanja and he ran away to the city. He made

238

a new home with some friends in a bus shelter. He would go to the rubbish tip with them each day to search through it for food and anything which he could sell.

After a week or so his skin became whitish and his head covered with sores. In a short time all the friends he stayed with had a skin disease. Other children showed them the way to a special shelter where they were able to get help.

Karanja stayed at the shelter for some months. It gave him somewhere to sleep and a few hours of classes each day. One day he found his younger brother with some older boys on the street. He didn't want his brother to live on the streets so he decided to take him back to their village where they both stayed on.

Understanding life on the streets

No two children are the same. Every single child who lives and works on the street needs to be treated as an individual.

For most children life on the streets is tiring and difficult. Many children have to combine work at home, at school and in the street and they enjoy few comforts. Many children do not like the discipline of school and together with the many other pressures on their time it is easy for them to drop out, and difficult for them to return. Some poor families depend on the children to help get a little extra money.

When they live or work on the street, children face a variety of dangers such as harassment, brutality, diseases, road accidents and harsh treatment by the police or other adults in the community. To protect themselves children often form groups. A group may have its own territory, rules, language, behavior, dress, hierarchy and games. The children may share food, stories, money, medicine and work. They may offer one another friendship, solidarity and support.

A group of children often has a leader and sometimes an adult protector. The leaders often exploit the children and teach them about the bad side of street life. They persuade children to engage in petty theft, prostitution and drug or solvent abuse. But the leaders can also offer security and support:

- ◆ "He advises me to be serious at home and in school."
- ◆ "When I'm sick, he sympathizes and buys me medicine."
- ◆ "He helps me out with the police."

- ◆ "When he has money he takes us to see the football [game]."
- ◆ "I usually sleep at the bus station with my younger sister and some other friends. Sometimes we go home. I cannot sleep for long. Everywhere it is dangerous. Especially for us girls." (Maria, 13 years)
- ◆ "Around six o'clock we go and sit in the park, talk about films, explain or describe some of the films that we've watched or just talk generally about funny, funny things and laugh." (Ahmed, 10 years)

Helping children who live or work on the street

Special activities to help children who live or work on the streets can take place in the community, at home, at school or at a special project base. It is best if the activities help children build up positive relationships with their families and community and give them self respect.

The jobs done by children in the street involve skills and special talents such as quick thinking, inventiveness, patience and common sense. The strong attachments which children can form help them learn about loyalty and solidarity. Children and

240

other people who want to help must build on these positive qualities.

Most children who live or work on the streets would welcome educational activities which allow them to earn at the same time. As the children are so independent, they need to be actively involved in planning activities. Let children suggest what they would like to do and help them to make choices. Help them learn to listen to each other, value other people's ideas and solve problems.

All activities should be relevant, even when the children plan to use their education as a way out of street life: reading material can come from everyday things like road signs, shop signs or newspapers; mathematics can be based on marketing skills.

Those working with these children need to respect, appreciate and encourage them. Nonformal educators need to work in a flexible and creative way. People who have experienced difficulties in their own childhood often make sympathetic educators.

Talk to adults who are important to the children; for instance their leaders or protectors. Getting the cooperation and assistance of those closest to the children will be the best way to help them.

In the community

People in the community need to understand that it is not the children's fault when they live or work on the streets. Instead of blaming the children and treating them as thieves and pests, people need to take positive steps both to help the children living or working on the streets and to prevent more children joining them.

Activities

Ideas for these activities have come from different parts of the world. They have helped children build links with people in the community.

- ◆ Community leaders have organized a place for children to meet together. Here the children sing, dance and play games. In some communities, special "after school clubs" are set up for children whose parents both work. They enjoy doing activities with their friends in a place where they feel cared for and protected.

♦ Young people have organized a place where children buy a cheap ticket to watch films. The "video shed" is a place where children make contact with people and groups who can help them with education, health or sports activities.

♦ Artisans have provided children with useful training. They help to build children's self confidence and develop positive attitudes.

♦ Health workers have organized workshops. Children who live or work in the streets know that health is important: illness makes them miserable and prevents them from earning money. The most common diseases for children who live or work on the street are skin diseases, stomach aches, diarrhea and pneumonia.

Groups of children participate in short workshops on health and then help to spread health messages to their friends.

♦ Scout groups have organized literacy clubs, recreational games and health and environment projects for parents and children. These joint activities help restore fragile relationships between children and adults in the community.

♦ Children have organized and run sport and organized games. Sports activities help strengthen the children's sense of discipline and earn them respect. They can bring children from different parts of a community together. Children take pride in these activities. They help to organize the activities and raise the money to keep them going.

At school

In a school where children are proud of the role they can play in helping one another, in spreading health messages to the community and in taking responsibility for their environment, there will be fewer difficulties with dropouts and vandalism.

Special activities in the classroom or at school can do a lot to help children who may be thinking about leaving home or school. Children in school can be made more aware of the dangers of street life; they can help to organize and run special activities for out-of-school children; they can encourage dropouts to return to school.

Activities

- ◆ Child-to-Child health activities link classroom activities with those in the community and home. These activities help to build children's confidence and make them feel useful and respected.
- ◆ Children who have faced the difficulties of life away from home and school can talk to other children about their experiences. Together they can write stories and songs and draw posters which can be used to raise awareness in the community. Concerts, competitions, exhibitions, parents days and open-days all help the community to become closer and develop a better understanding of the needs of the school and its children.
- ◆ In some schools special Child-to-Child committees have been set up. They include the head teacher, other teachers and senior pupils. The committees can plan ways to help vulnerable children in the school and the community.

The committees can help to run special "catch-up clubs," to find children who have dropped out, and encourage them to return to school without shame. Children in the top primary classes can become the "catch-up club" teachers and help children to catch up with school work they have missed.

◆ Sports activities can involve children who do not go to school. They can be included in teams or be invited to train or play regularly with school-going children.

At home

Poverty and ill health can lead to many tensions in a child's home. Parents and other children at home can try to help each other understand the reasons behind these difficulties and try to work out their problems in a positive way.

In our story, Karanja learned that escaping from his home for a life on the streets was not going to solve his family's problems.

Activities

◆ If a child is being bad-tempered and aggressive at home, other children and adults can try to find out what is wrong (children are often better at doing this). Try to think of things the child can do for the rest of the family which will make him or her feel important and useful.

◆ Parents whose children have a happy home and school life can teach them to care for and respect children who are worse off. If a child of a "poor relation" is brought into a family, he or she should be treated with as much respect as the other children.

◆ Children often find elderly people easy to talk to. They can often form important friendships. Elderly people enjoy talking to children and telling them stories which teach them about their culture and traditions. This helps to build a child's sense of belonging to a family and a community.

◆ Children can make toys to sell or for playing with younger children: footballs, juggling balls, toy cars, toy bicycles and so on. Parents and others in the community can make scraps available and encourage toymaking projects.

CHILDREN'S RIGHTS

EVERYONE IN THE COMMUNITY NEEDS TO SHOUT LOUDLY ABOUT CHILDREN'S RIGHTS. MANY GOVERNMENTS HAVE COMMITTED THEMSELVES TO IMPROVE LIFE FOR CHILDREN AND PROTECT THEIR RIGHTS. MANY ARE FAILING TO DO SO.

SOME COUNTRIES HAVE ORGANISED 'CHILDREN'S HEARINGS' WHERE CHILDREN ARE HELPED TO VOICE THEIR OPINION IN PUBLIC ABOUT ISSUES THAT CONCERN THEM. FIND OUT IF THIS IS SO IN YOUR COUNTRY. HELP PEOPLE IN THE COMMUNITY UNDERSTAND MORE ABOUT CHILDREN'S RIGHTS. THE CHILDREN WILL HELP.

★ ORGANISE POSTER CAMPAIGNS, MARCHES, CHILDREN'S HEARINGS.

★ ENCOURAGE CHILDREN TO SPEAK ON THE RADIO, ON TELEVISION AND AT PUBLIC MEETINGS.

At a special project base

A special project for children living or working on the streets can be a useful "go-between" for the children, their families, schools and community. It is unhelpful for projects to provide special short term services which separate the children from people in the community who can give them the long term support they need.

Activities

- ◆ Projects can link artisans with children to teach them income-generating skills: soap making, market gardening, poultry keeping. Children can find people they like to help them.
- ◆ Children, parents, teachers, employers and community members can use the project base to discuss problems with a project worker.
- ◆ Children and project workers can work together to make contact with their families and start rebuilding family relationships.

245

- ◆ Children who have budgeting skills can help less experienced children learn to save and plan.
- ◆ Projects can organize special recreation programs (sports, music, drama, crafts) which also include children living at home and going to school.
- ◆ Children are good at expressing themselves through theater, music and dance. Some street children earn their living through street performances such as puppet shows, acrobatics and juggling, singing and bands. Performances help to make communities aware of the needs of these children in a way that also earns the children respect. Projects can help and encourage the children to do this.

Follow-up activities

- ◆ Children can find out how many children dropped out of school before, during and after the special activities were introduced to help prevent dropouts.
- ◆ Children can try to find out what has happened to children who dropped out of their class.
- ◆ Children can find out what other children learned when they went to a health workshop, a games club or a literacy class.
- ◆ Children can find out what the "little teachers" and their students are doing at the "catch up club." They can find out from the school teachers how the "catch up clubs" have helped the students and the "little teachers" and what the problems are.
- ◆ Children can find out about the attitudes of community members towards children living and working on the street before and after a special "awareness campaign."

NOTE

1   This appendix is based on Child-to-Child Activity Sheet 8.1. Child-to-Child activity sheets are a resource for teachers, and health and community workers. They are designed to help children understand how to improve health in other children, their families and their communities. Topics chosen are

important for community health and suit the age, interests and experience of children. The text, ideas and activities may be freely adapted to suit local conditions. A publications list is available from: The Child-to-Child Trust, The Institute of Education, 20, Bedford Way, London WC1H OAL United Kingdom.

Appendix B: Resources

MISSION AGENCIES WORKING WITH STREET CHILDREN:
A SAMPLER

ACTION International U.S.A.
Mr. Doug Nichols, International Director
P.O. Box 490
Bothell, WA 98041-0490 U.S.A.
Phone: (206)485-1967
Fax: (206)486-9477

The Arms of Jesus Children's Mission, Inc.
Dr. Sam Martin, Director
1848 Liverpool Road, Suite 160, Unit 9
Pickering, Ontario L1V 6M3 Canada
Fax: (905)509-6141

Child Evangelism Fellowship, Inc.
Rev. Reese R. Kauffman, President
P.O. Box 348
Warrenton, MO 63383-0348 U.S.A.
Phone: (314)456-4321
Fax: (314)456-2078

Careforce International, Canada
Resource and networking mission
Rev. James Wilson, International President
1100 Burloak Drive
Burlington, Ontario L7L 6B2 Canada
Phone: (905)319-3555
Fax: (905)319-3557

Careforce International, U.S.A.
Resource and networking mission
Dr. Ernest Taylor, Executive Vice President
P.O. Box 151322
Cape Coral, FL 33915-1322 U.S.A.
(Phone and Fax same as for Canada office)

Compassion International, Inc.
Dr. Wesley Stafford, President
13955 Cragwood Drive
Colorado Springs, CO 80918 U.S.A.
Phone: (719)594-9900
Fax: (719)594-6271

Dorcas Aid International
Mr. Ken Sweers, Chief Executive Officer
6475 28th Street S.E., Suite 233
Grand Rapids, MI 49546 U.S.A.
Phone: (616)363-5860
Fax: (616)454-3456

Heart of the Father Outreach
Mr. & Mrs. John Moritz, Directors
P.O. Box 491
Undermountain Road
Sheffield, MA 01257 U.S.A.
Phone: (413)229-2922
Fax: (413)229-3257

Homeless Children International, Inc.
Mr. David M. High, President
P.O. Box 53026
Knoxville, TN 37950 U.S.A.
Phone: (423)558-9099

In His Arms
Kim Burr Turnbull, Director
P.O. Box 820864
Vicksburg, MS 39182 U.S.A.
Phone & Fax: (601)638-4488

Kids Alive! International
Alfred R. Lacky, President
2507 Cumberland Drive
Valparaiso, IN 46383 U.S.A.
Phone: (219)464-9035
Fax: (219)462-5611

Latin America Mission, Inc.
Dr. David Howard, President
P.O. Box 52-7900
Miami, FL 33152 U.S.A.
Phone: (305)884-8400
Fax: (305)885-8649

Metro Ministries
Rev. Bill Wilson
P.O. Box 370695
Brooklyn, NY 11237-0015 U.S.A.
Phone: (718)453-3352

Oakseed Ministries International
Mr. Ed Bradley, President
P.O. Box 11222
Burke, VA 22009 U.S.A.
Phone: (703)455-2652
Fax: (703)455-3904

SIM International
Dr. Jim Pluddeman
P.O. Box 7900
Charlotte, NC 28241-7900 U.S.A.
Phone: (704)588-4300
Fax: (704)587-1518

Rainbows of Hope
(A Ministry of WEC International)
Dr. Phyllis Kilbourn, Director
P.O. Box 1707
Fort Washington, PA 19034 U.S.A.
Phone: (215)646-2323, ex. 101
Fax: (215)646-6202

UFM International
Dr. James H. Nesbitt, General Director
P.O. Box 306
Bala Cynwyd, PA 19004 U.S.A.
Phone: (215)667-7660
Fax: (215)660-9068

The Viva Network
Mr. Patrick McDonald, International Coordinator
P.O. Box 633
Oxford, OX1 4YP England
Phone: 44-1865-450-800
Fax: 44-1865-203-567

World Vision, Inc.
Dr. Robert A. Seiple, President
P.O. Box 9716
Federal Way, WA 98063-9716 U.S.A.
Phone: (206)815-1000
Fax: (206)815-3140

Youth with a Mission (YWAM)
Mr. Loren Cunningham, International Director
Mr. Steve Goode, Director of Mercy Ships International
GPO Box 177
Bangkok 10501 Thailand

Resource Books

Anderson, Jeff, ed. *Crisis on the Streets: A Ministry Guide for Taking the Street out of Street Children*. Action International.

Anderson, Neil T. and Steve Russo. *The Seduction of Our Children*. Harvest House Publishers.

Aptekar, Lewis. *Street Children of Cali*. Duke University Press. (Detailed study of street children in one Colombian city.)

Blanc, Cristina Szanton Blanc, ed. *Urban Children in Distress*. UNICEF.

Butcher, Andy. *Street Children: The Tragedy and Challenge of the World's Millions of Modern-Day Oliver Twist*. Nelson Word Publishing.

Dallape, Fabio. *An Experience with Street Children.* Undugu Society of Kenya (P.O. Box 40417 Nairobi, Kenya 1987).

Dimenstein, Gilberto. *Brazil: War on Children.* Latin America Bureau. (Investigation of the truth behind the 'death squad' reports.)

Ennew, Judith and Brian Milne. *The Next Generation: Lives of Third World Children.* Zed Books. (Wide-ranging review of the social and economic issues confronting children in the developing world.)

Grigg, Viv. *Companion to the Poor.* Monrovia, California: MARC, 1990. (Christian perspective on mission among the poor and needy.)

Grigg, Viv. *Cry of the Urban Poor.* Monrovia, California: MARC, 1992.

Kilbourn, Phyllis, ed. *Children in Crisis: A New Commitment.* Monrovia, California: MARC, 1996.

Strobel, Charles F. *Room in the Inn: Ways Your Congregation Can Help Homeless People.* Nashville, Tennessee: Abingdon Press.

Swart, Jill. *Malunde: The Street Children of Hillbrow.* Johannesburg: University of South Africa. (Research study of street children in Johannesburg.)

Vittachi, Anuradha. *Stolen Childhood.* Polity Press.

Wilson, Bill. *Whose Child Is This?* New York: Metro Ministries.

JOURNAL ARTICLES AND REPORTS

Agnelli, Susanna. Mid-1980s overview report by Committee of the Independent Commission on International Humanitarian issues. Wiedenfeld.

Dorcas Aid, "Street Children International Directory." Dorcas Aid, P.O. Box 12, 1619 ZG Andijk, The Netherlands. Guide to many Christian ministries working among street children around the world.

Junker-Kenny, Maureen and Norbert Mette, eds. Concilium, "Little Children Suffer" (1996, No. 2). Maryknoll, New York: Orbis.

Urban Mission. March 1992, Volume 9, Number 4. Articles and case studies on street children.

CURRICULUM AND TRAINING

Jubilee Action, a Christian-based advocacy group taking action for the suffering church worldwide, produces "Street Life," a complete training module on street children. "Street Life" is a superb resource for schools, youth groups and workshops containing high school level student work sheets with professionally-researched lesson plans, mini-posters, world map, photos and more. For further information contact Jubilee Action, St. John's, Cranleigh Road, Wonersh, Guildford, England GU5 OQX; fax (01483)894797.

Child Evangelism Fellowship (see address under mission agency listing): Summer Urban Ministries; practical training and experience in evangelizing and ministering to children in the inner city.

Youth With A Mission has a training course, Children in Need. This is an intense three month child worker training program. The training focuses on helping/counseling sexually, physically and emotionally abused children and the disabled child. Information can be obtained from Mr. Richard Birkebak, co-director, Y.W.A.M. Urban Ministries, P.O. Box 75145, Seattle, WA 98125.

VIDEOS

Missing. An evangelistic and family-viewing drama about a street boy in Manila. Available with discussion materials on church loan from Gospel Films, 2735 East Apple Avenue, Muskegon, MI 49442.

The Wild Side. Presents America's mission field in the inner city. Walk through the ghettos with Metro Ministries staff (Metro Ministries, 1-800-462-7770).

Shalom Bombay. An award-winning drama about the lives of street children in Bombay. Shot entirely on location with key roles filled by real-life street kids. Available from Mirabel Films on video rental basis.

**MARC**

Bringing you key resources on the world mission of the church

MARC books and other publications support the work of MARC (Mission Advanced Research and Communications Center), which is to inspire vision and empower Christian mission among those who extend the whole gospel to the whole world.

Also by Phyllis Kilbourn:

▶ *Healing the Children of War.* A practical handbook for ministry to children who have suffered deep traumas. Examines the impact of war on children; the grieving child; forgiveness; restoring hope to the child; and many other important issues that surround children who have been victimized by war. $21.95

▶ *Children in Crisis: A New Commitment.* Alerts you to the multiple ways in which children are suffering around the world—AIDS, abandonment, abuse, forced labor, girl child—and equips you to respond in biblical ways. $21.95

Other recent titles from MARC include:

▶ *Serving With the Poor in Africa: Cases in Holistic Ministry,* T. Yamamori, B. Myers, K. Bediako & L. Reed editors. Real holistic ministry cases are presented from throughout Africa. Commentary and analysis on such topics as holistic healing, AIDS and evangelism deepens your understanding of holism. $15.95

▶ *With an Eye on the Future: Development and Mission in the 21st Century,* Duane Elmer and Lois McKinney, editors. Cutting-edge thinkers present essays in the fields of mission, development and church leadership that propose new strategies in the areas that will be vital to mission in the next century. $24.95

▶ *The New Context of World Mission* by Bryant L. Myers. A thorough yet concise visual portrayal of the entire sweep of Christian mission. Full-color graphics and up-to-date statistics show you where mission has been and where it's heading.

Book... $ 8.95
Slides... $149.95
Overheads....................................... $149.95
Presentation Set *(one book, slides and overheads)* $249.00

Order Toll Free in USA: 1-800-777-7752
Direct: (818) 301-7720

MARC A division of World Vision
800 W. Chestnut Ave. • Monrovia • CA • 91016-3198 • USA

Ask for the MARC Newsletter and complete publications list